THE BAR BAND

SURVIVAL

GUIDE

Printed in the United States of America

First Printing 2015

House of Mystery Productions

ISBN-13: 978-0692352281
ISBN-10: 0692352287

Ordering Information:
Quantity sales: Special discounts are available on quantity purchases by corporations, associations, and others. For details, contact the author by visiting www.bandsurvivalguide.com

The

Bar Band

Survival Guide

by

Allen Lighthiser

To Michael Doane who's still living the dream...rock on brother

Table of Contents

The Bar Band Survival Guide - An Introduction

So, you want to start a band. When you get right down to it, it's not too hard to find a couple of guys who want to hang out in a garage all day, drink some beer and try to play "Stairway To Heaven". Likewise, the world is full of people who want to be the next Justin Bieber or Madonna (is she still a relevant example?) spending money on studio time laying down tracks that no one will ever hear. If you are looking to do anything like that, I probably can't help you. There are other resources available for stuff like that. I want this one to be different...

If you want to make MONEY playing music, then this is another thing entirely. In order to be successful, you will need several things; gear, time, dedication, good song selection, marketing skills and good musicians to be in your band. I can help point you in the right direction on most of these topics, but there are other things you will have to provide on your own. The biggest one here is, of course, talent. Before deciding to venture out and start your own band, do make sure that you are actually able to play your instrument. We have enough bad music floating around.

After talent, the next most important thing is managing your expectations. You will notice that the title of this book is *The Bar Band Survival Guide*, and not *How to get on the MTV* or something like that. What I'm talking about is being a working musician...someone who's out there in the trenches living the life, having a great time and making some serious jingle. You may very well turn out to be the next Aerosmith, but you have to start somewhere. We always called it a "bar band" because that's mainly where we ended up playing. If you don't dig the bar scene, there are plenty of other venue options out there. Trust me. Follow this guide, and you will have your pick.

For the last fifteen years, I have been a member of a ton of different bands ranging in genre from classic and modern rock to country, polka, punk and more. Some of these esteemed groups included Day Thirteen, Shark Sandwich, Not A Few and most notably the Seattle Seven. That was me. Me and six other guys. Anyhow, you get the point. You have never heard of any of these groups. We were never as famous as the Foo Fighters or as bad as the Insane Clown Posse. That was ok though, because we accomplished our main mission, which was to make good money by doing something we loved; playing music.

There are too many people out there who want to play music for money, but don't end up giving it a shot because they either lack the confidence or don't know how to get started. Make no mistake about it...starting a band that doesn't suck, plays music you enjoy and gets paid for it all at the same time isn't easy, but it is doable. While I was in high school and college, I was playing out twice a week, making anywhere from 200.00 to 400.00 for eight hours of work on the weekend. That was just me. The other guys in the band were making the same amount too. We had fun doing it, and most of the time we were still awake and unloading gear until the sun came up. It usually took the rest of the week to get my hearing back, but I loved every minute of it.

Doing this will make you into a good musician. Even if you are already a pretty solid player, you will improve. Playing live music, no matter how well rehearsed, is always full of surprises. In these situations, you will either sink or swim...swooping into an unexpected guitar lead because the other guys amp blew up or doing another chorus or two because the bass player is passed out from drinking too much Jack mixed with those pain meds he bought from the sound guy. You will want to avoid having people like this guy in your band by the way, but we will get to that in a bit. Crazy stuff happens, and it will be a learning experience. Plus, you will be guaranteed to have great stories for the rest of your life.

What I have for you here on the following pages is absolutely everything that I have learned over my many years of playing shows at county fairs, private parties, weddings, retirement homes, biker rallies and of course bars (just to name a few). You are going to get everything from the ground up. What kind of band to start, where to find musicians, what gear to get, how to select songs, how to manage yourself and more. It isn't always pretty. I have included some personal stories to help illustrate my points, and maybe prevent you from making some of the same mistakes I have made. I was lucky to learn from some successful bandleaders, and some who were not so successful. Sometimes learning how NOT to do things is much more effective and leaves a longer lasting impression.

By the end of this book, I believe that you will have the tools and knowledge you need to enter the very competitive world of live music entertainment and come out on top. We are going to start out with the basics. Even if you kind of already know what you are doing, check it out anyway and don't skip ahead...maybe you will learn something new. If you are the kind of musician who cares enough about their craft to go out and by a book like this, you are already ahead of the game. You can do this. Stick with me here...

That's how it always starts...very small.

Part I. - Getting the Band (Back) Together

Jake: We're putting the band back together.

Mr. Fabulous: Forget it. No way.

Elwood: We're on a mission from God.

The Blues Brothers - 1980

Initial Considerations

Before you start down the road on any of this stuff, you need to check yourself. No, really. Are you capable of being a bandleader? I'm just the guy writing this book, so I can ask the tough questions. In order to be in a band that goes out and makes cash, in real competition with other bands, you gotta be good. Whether you are a musician who can read music or not, you are going to have to learn to play by ear. This might actually be the biggest thing there is when it comes to assembling a working band. You are going to have to learn a whole bunch of songs, and at a pretty quick pace in order to stay relevant...constantly updating your repertoire to keep crowds interested. If you haven't already gotten to this point, start working on that now. Go ahead. I'll wait.

All set? Good. My reasoning here is the fact that in order to be successful, you are going to have to put together a pretty stellar lineup. As one may imagine, it's always easier to get other good people to play with you when you are already pretty talented yourself. Talented musicians are always in high demand, and they tend to not waste too much time on projects that they don't see going anywhere. So the better you are, the better you can expect your band to be. This is an area where you are going to see quite a return on investment, with the investment of course being your overall effort and skill.

This leads us to the next question. How many musicians should you be looking for, and what instruments should they play? If you don't sing yourself, should you hire a singer? There are several factors to consider when asking this question. First of all, no matter how many people you add, you should try to establish a solid core right from the start. This means filling the three absolutely necessary positions. These are of course guitar, bass and drums. Without these three instruments, you don't really have a band.

For most of my playing career, and in any band I managed myself, I have always tried to keep numbers to a minimum. The reasons for this are quite simple. First of all, if you are going to be playing with two or more people in your group, it's going to be absolutely imperative to get along with everyone. For each additional person you bring in, you dramatically increase your chances of not getting along, as well as the difficulty level when it comes to managing the group in general. At the same time, you are lowering your own income. It doesn't take an accountant to figure out that no matter how much money you make in a night, the fewer people you have to split it up with the more everyone will get.

With that being said, adding more musicians who play unique or hard to find instruments can increase the pool of songs from which you can draw, enabling you to reach a larger audience. If you can reach more people, it's quite possible you can make more money. Some unique instruments may include a keyboard or second guitarist for classic rock or dance, or a steel guitar or fiddle for country. You would probably want to consider how often these instruments would be used in your set before making any decisions. A fiddle may be incredible if you want to play "The Devil Went Down to Georgia", but it's probably not worth the investment if that's the only song you play where it's needed.

To get started, just try to fill the three core positions. The most successful groups that I have been involved with only had these three basic instruments. We all sang either lead or harmony vocals as well, which made everything sound fuller and somewhat made up for a lack of instrumentation. If you are going to go this route, however, your guitar player needs to be pretty good; knowing when he can go into leads with only the bass and drums backing him up. If he doesn't know how to do this properly, things can quickly begin to sound like an empty, scattered mess. If you have any doubts at all on this, it may be worth the trouble to pick up a rhythm guitar player in addition to someone who can play lead.

One of the things you should really try to avoid is hiring a singer that doesn't do anything else. Trust me, there are a ton of people out there who just want to walk in with a microphone and pretend they know that they're doing. I call these guys "Karaoke All-Stars". Even if they are an excellent singer, in a situation where you are trying to make the most money possible, they should really be bringing something else to the table. Rhythm guitar is a great instrument to stick your main vocalist on. Usually, chording to fill in the background is pretty basic and leaves plenty of room for them to concentrate on singing. If you have someone who can't do these two things at once, you probably want to steer clear.

Another reason to avoid someone who is "just a singer" (or vocalist as they often times like to be called) is because if they don't know how to play an instrument, this should set off some warning signs. Somewhere along the way, your band will very likely find itself in a situation where you want to play a song, but may have to change the key. Most of the time, the band members change the key to accommodate the singer. Sometimes though, the singer needs to do this to accommodate the band. One reason for this could be needing to have certain instruments drop tuned and not having the time to change them all. Another may just be that with your current lineup, a song just doesn't sound right due to instrumentation (or lack thereof) and needs to be changed to sound better. Someone who doesn't know anything about actually playing music and how key changes work is not going to be able to do this properly. They might manage for a line or two, but see what happens about 30 seconds into the song.

Where To Start Looking

Ok, so you know what type of musicians you are looking to hire, but where do you find these people? Finding the right people who are not only talented but also fit into the group can sometimes be a long, frustrating process. You may even hire several different people only to find out later on that things aren't working out for whatever reason. More often than not, these things happen at the most inconvenient moments possible. With this in mind, it's always smart to have a list of people, known as fill-ins, who specialize in stepping up at a moments notice and are able to learn large lists of songs very quickly.

Here are some common places you can find musicians looking for work. We will take a look at each one individually:

- Newspapers
- Craigslist
- Musician Finder Websites
- Bulletin Boards
- Music Stores
- Music Teachers
- Jam Sessions

Newspapers

Back in the day, a lot of people actually read the classifieds section of the newspaper, and it was a pretty good place to look for just about anything you needed from used waffle irons and stuffed moose heads to karate lessons and bass players. Some people still read these, and many newspapers even post this section online in addition to printing it in their physical paper. All you have to do is call the newspaper and ask to take out an ad in the "Help Wanted" section. You might be surprised at the amount of responses you will get. You will pay by the line, but the cost is very low.

The ad in the paper should be brief, but clearly state the specific type of musician you want to hire, the type of music you play, and most importantly the fact that it is a paying gig (it is, isn't it?). A sample ad might look something like this:

GUITAR PLAYER WANTED: Working classic rock band is searching for a solid lead guitar player. Gigs lined up through October. Must have experience and be willing to work as a team. Must have your own gear. No egos or drugs. Check us out at myband.com or call Dave. 304-123-4567

The no drugs thing here is actually pretty important depending on the type of environment you wish to foster. Unfortunately, the music world, just like the regular world, is full of people with problems. Ok, maybe "problems" are a little more prevalent in the music world (See Jimi Hendrix, Kurt Cobain, Miley Cyrus etc.). You should not be afraid to come right out and ask questions about whether a potential candidate for your group is drug-free and/or if they are able to control how much alcohol they drink. Having a few drinks at a show, especially since they are often on the house, is normal. Getting drunk and falling over on stage and causing the show to stop or get cancelled is not. Avoid this problem from the start by not hiring addicts or alcoholics.

Craigslist

This day in age, everyone is pretty familiar with Craigslist. Using this website, you can pretty much find anything you are looking for, and a ton of things no one should be looking for, ever. Site navigation is straightforward and simple, and you need only click on your state and specific location to get started and post in the correct spot. Luckily for us, Craigslist has a specific category for musicians, which pretty much insures that your ad will receive a ton of relevant traffic. On top of that, posting on Craigslist is absolutely free.

When writing your ad, you can do it in the same format as the prior example. Unlike the newspaper though, you don't have to pay by the line here, so feel free to give more information. With the unlimited room, some things to consider adding might be photos of your existing band or your logo, a list of songs you already play or hope to play, or an influences section. Influences are always nice to list since they help the reader get a good idea of what you are going for specifically. Also, don't forget to add a link to your website if you have one, or at least a page where sound samples or recordings of your band can be heard. If you don't have any of these things yet, don't worry. Check out the coming sections on marketing and demos and you will be good to go.

This should probably go without saying, but anytime you are meeting people from the internet (or anywhere else, for that matter), please use common sense and caution. There are a ton of freaks and weirdos out there, so try to make your first meeting with someone in a public area. After you have used your keen skills of perception to determine they are not trying to kill you or lock you in their basement, it's probably safe to invite them to your practice space for a try out. If they turn out to be a freak show, call the police.

Musician Finder Websites

In a world where a Smurf ashtray is just three clicks away, it shouldn't surprise us that there are some websites that exist solely to bring musicians together. I have used these over the years to some moderate success, but they are probably my least favorite option on this list.

Even so, you should give them a shot and see if they work for you. The good news is, most of them are free and accounts are not generally difficult to set up. Since the Internet is constantly changing, any sites that I recommend could quite possibly be obsolete by the time you read this. Just try doing a search on Google for "musician finder". At the time of this writing, some of the better-known sites include:

themusicianfinder.com (Owned by Guitar Center)
bandmix.com (One of the better ones out there)
bandfinder.com (Haven't tried this one, but it seems fairly popular)

Sites like these often include sections for you to fill out a biography, list the members that are currently in your band, upload pictures and sound samples, and of course a spot to tell people what kind of musicians you are currently searching for to complete your band. Since people can respond by e-mail, this might be a good alternative for those who would like to get to know someone a little bit before giving away their number or having to call the other person up on the phone.

Bulletin Boards

This is definitely one of my favorite ways to find another musician. Have you ever been in one of those old, run down, dirty gas stations where some guy covered in grease with his name stitched onto his shirt pumps your gas for you? Believe it or not, these are one of the most likely places to find what some people refer to as a "community bulletin board". I'm sure you have seen these things before...most of the time they will be littered with business cards from psychics and pet sitting services. This is a perfect place to advertise your current vacancy, and maybe even find a flyer from some other musician who happens to be looking for work.

The best way to go about this is to make a flyer using whatever word processing software you have on your computer. Microsoft Word, Word Perfect or Pages will work great for this. If you don't have access to any of these, try downloading Open Office, as it is a nice alternative to the bigger brands, and available online for free. Once you open up your software, start a new document and look around for template options. Search for one that says "flyer" or something similar.

Most programs have an option that will make you a template with those little tear off tags on the bottom of the paper. These are by far the best option you can go for since people don't have to have a pen to write your number down. It also makes it less likely that someone will rip the thing off the wall and walk away with it. Just make sure that when you are telling the computer what to put on the tags, you remember to list not only the phone number, but also the name of the band or a contact person. This makes it a bit more comfortable for people to contact you, since it can be a little weird to call someone up whose number they found on a corkboard outside a bathroom.

You will want the main section of the flyer to contain all the pertinent information that you would put in any ad like those that we discussed prior. In addition to that, you will want to add something that makes the ad stick out on the board so people don't think it's just another ad for a puppy mill or something. The best way to do that is to put a huge picture of a guitar, music note or something else that identifies the paper with music right in the middle of the page. In the past, I have created my own images to get attention on a crowded board. My favorite one was a picture of a milk carton with the caption "Missing. Have you seen our guitar player?" and had a blacked out silhouette of a face on the side. You are an artist, after all. Be creative.

Music Stores

If I were looking for a fireman, I would probably check the fire station. If I had only fifteen minutes to locate a clown, I would look for the nearest circus. Why should it be any different with musicians? If you need to find one, you could do worse than looking in a music store. More often than not, music stores are chock-full of people sitting around testing out instruments and browsing for equipment. Head on down to your local retailer and have a look around. Quite frequently, the guys who work there are very likely working musicians themselves, and are probably pretty good at it. Even if they are not personally looking for a gig, they may very well be able to call up someone they know who is.

These places will also probably have bulletin boards like the ones we just talked about. These are usually just for musicians though, and will most likely be riddled with people looking for work. Sometimes a DJ's business card will find it's way up there, but those are usually spotted quickly and thrown in the trash by employees or concerned citizens. Check the board for phone numbers or leave an ad of your own. Once again, putting a flyer up here will cost you nothing but time and will be displayed right in front of your target audience.

Music Teachers

Another great way to find a new band mate is to get a hold of the phone book or do an online search for music teachers in your area. If you are looking for a drummer, find someone who teaches drums and call them up. Explain your situation including what kind of music you play, how experienced the band is and maybe even what the average gig with your band will pay. Chances are, the teacher will have no problem finding one of their students who is eager to join a working band to gain valuable experience. Who knows? You may even find that the teacher wouldn't mind picking up another gig on the side.

Jam Sessions

If you can find a good one, I firmly believe that jam sessions are by far the best way to find likeminded and able musicians to join your group. If you have never participated in one of these, I would encourage you to seek out an opportunity to do so as soon as possible. This is probably something that you should have a lot of experience doing prior to starting your own band, and we will be talking about them quite a bit in upcoming chapters.

If you are not familiar with them, jam sessions work like this. A bar or club (often times a place like an American Legion or VFW) will hire a band to come in and set up their equipment. This band is referred to as the "house band", and will often start out the night by playing a few songs or maybe even half a set with their regular group before inviting other people up to the stage to play. Guitar and bass players sometimes bring their own instruments and sometimes not, but larger and more awkward equipment like drums, amps and keyboards are always provided by the house band. In the event that not a lot of people want to get up and play, the band is prepared to play all night by themselves if they have to.

One of the great things about jams is the fact that you can play a few songs with a person before you even bring up the subject of needing someone for your group. You can spend the whole night at the club listening to various players, pick out your favorite ones and talk with them. More often than not, people who go to these things are looking for a new gig or something to do on the side in addition to their main project. Also, if you need to gain some experience playing live but don't yet have a band together, there is no better place to get your start.

The jam session atmosphere is generally very inviting and open to musicians of all experience levels. I started playing at these things when I was 15 years old, and have gotten some of the best advice on music I've ever heard at them. I also ended up meeting my best friend for over ten years at a jam. I was in a band where we were looking for a new bass player. Go figure.

If you don't have anyone organizing anything like this in your area, you may consider making the effort to start one yourself. Find a nice club or bar that has a stage and ask them if they are open to the idea. You may need to provide the equipment, but some places even have their own stuff. If you do decide to start your own jam night, do it for a month or two and just wait and see how many bizarre stories you have. It's a great deal of fun, and the musicians in your area will thank you.

Time for Tryouts

Ok, so now you've made flyers, called the newspapers, posted on Craigslist and opened a few profiles on musician finder websites. You know that the phone is going to be ringing soon, but what do you tell these guys when they call? What kind of stuff do you need to know to make sure they are the right individual for the job, or are going to be a good fit in the existing group you already have (if you have one)? For the purposes of what we'll cover here, we are going to suppose you are looking for a bass player. Just substitute whatever instrument you are actually looking for.

You will most likely get calls from lots of people, so you will probably want to jot down the details from your phone calls or e-mails so that you'll be able to tell these guys apart. If you have done everything right up until this point, they should have a pretty good idea of what you are looking for since you were pretty detailed in the ads you placed. If they have any additional questions, and they probably will, now is a pretty good time to answer them.

In order to start scheduling bassists for tryouts, you should develop a list of three or four songs that you and the drummer know very well. They should probably be the same songs for each person you have come in to play, so they can just walk in and you can get things going. You will want to select some cover songs that are readily available somewhere online. This day in age, YouTube is a musician's best friend. Once you give them the names of the songs, they should have no problem looking them up if they have to learn them. If they say they already know them, then that works too.

Before scheduling a date and time, make sure to ask questions about anything you think might be a potential issue. If you want to avoid hiring someone who drinks too much or takes drugs, don't be afraid to ask this up front. You don't have to be a jackass about it, but you can try saying something like "we like to keep things professional, so we keep drinking to a minimum. Is that ok with you?" Another way to go about it is something like "you know, the last guy we had playing bass for us ended up falling over on the stage from being really drunk and taking a handful of drugs, so we want to try to avoid that this time. Is that cool with you?" This very situation will probably happen to you at least once or twice if you play live music for any length of time, but if you have to, just make it up for now and see what they say.

Another question you will absolutely need to ask is whether or not they have their own equipment. Anyone calling who is trying to play bass in a band better damn well at least have a bass. What they might not have though, is a suitable amplifier for what you are looking to do. If all they have is a small practice amp, they are probably going to need to get something bigger before they will be able to play bars and clubs. If you have an amp sitting around the practice room for them to use, that's great. Many bands have some old gear in their practice space so everyone doesn't have to haul drums and amps around, but you probably don't want to be bringing stuff back and forth to shows for them all the time.

At this point, you should go ahead and schedule them in for a try out. You can get a whole lineup of people all in one day, or you can spread them all out over however long you need. I find that having them all come over on one day with about an hour and a half in between applicants is ideal. This way, if you get someone who's really terrible, you are only stuck with them for a limited period of time, and can get rid of them without making things awkward by telling them that the next guy is coming in. Additionally, it really sucks to have to set up all that gear for just one guy, play four songs and then call it a day.

While you are evaluating these players, there are a few different things you should be looking for besides just playing ability. Here are just a few: How comfortable are they with their instrument? Do they look excited about playing and actually want to be there? Are they the kind of person you think you can stand being around for hours and hours at a time? Do they just play their instrument, or are they willing to sing? (Bringing other stuff to the table is always great). Are they organized and appear to have a good work ethic?

If you pay attention to all of these things, you can probably make a pretty fair judgment about someone. Whatever you do, don't just automatically decide to go with the first guy you try out, now matter how talented he may be. Don't be afraid to give it a shot with some of the other people you have talked to and see how they pan out. Once you do decide you may have found the right player though, you will want to ask them some final questions before you welcome them into the fold.

At this point, you will want to make sure that your practice schedule will work for the new guy, and that's he's willing to make the commitment long term. Going through the process of finding a musician is a long and time-consuming one. Even worse, you will very likely not be able to play live during this time, and will have to wait around for someone new to learn the set list before you can go back out and make money. Trust me, you will want to make the best decision you can the first time around. This is not to say that these guys will necessarily stick around forever, but it's worth it to make every effort to only take on individuals who are serious and have good intentions.

You will also want to let the guy know how often you plan on playing out and make sure that works for him. Some people only want to play shows once or twice a month. Others want to play only on the weekends, and some are looking to play all week long and as often as possible. While any of these scenarios that work for you are just fine, you will want to make sure that everyone is on the same page before making any commitments. Additionally, you will want to discuss the areas in which you plan on playing. Do you want to play only local clubs? Just the tri-state area? Do you have a bus and are looking to travel up and down the coast? These things can factor in big time to someone's decision to join a group, so it's only right to let them know ahead of time. Figuring all of this out right now will save a lot of hassle in the long run.

Part II. - Laying the Groundwork

Start a band...

Scrape up some money, buy a van..

Learn Freebird and Ramblin' Man..

Never buy another beer again...

Brad Paisley, 2008

Developing a Set List

After you find the right musicians for your band, you are going to need to start rehearsing as soon as possible. We are going to get into the finer points of practice later on, but for now, let's figure out what it is that you are going to play. Undoubtedly, you have already picked out a genre and have some idea of the songs you want to play. At this point though, you need to figure out specifics.

First of all, you are going to need to determine if you are going to be playing covers or originals. Since you have picked up this book and are presumably interested in making money, my guess is that you are going to be playing mostly cover songs. I realize that there are going to be some readers who will be appalled by this thought, but hear me out. To be as blunt as possible, nobody in the venues you will likely be playing wants to hear or hire you to play a full night of original songs. It just isn't going to happen.

Before you flip out, start smashing things and try to look up where I live, please notice that I said "full night of original songs." If your band has some original work that you would like to add in, then by all means, feel free to do so. The goal though, is to kind of slip these songs in without making a huge deal about it. The biggest compliment you can get in a situation like this is when someone comes up to you after the show and tells you they really liked that one song you did, but can't recall the name. If you do it this way, the audience will be more apt to listen with an open mind, rather than assuming your original music will be terrible. I know it sucks, but this is just how people are.

In my experience, I've found it's usually best to work in two or three original tunes a night if you have them. Try to place one in each set after the first set, so everyone in the audience is settled in and your listenability has been established with well-known numbers. You can put them in discreetly or openly announce, "this one is an original." If you keep things in moderation and the songs are good enough, you will be surprised how often people will request them at later shows. This can be a big boost later on for selling your own albums with original material.

So at this point you will need to establish a list of songs that you will be playing in every show. If you are doing a show in a bar or club, the common hours are either 10 PM to 2 AM or 9 PM to 1 AM. That's FOUR hours of space that you and your band will need to cover. I know it sounds like a lot (and it is), but with proper planning and practice, you will be able to handle it. Before you choose the actual songs, you are going to need to determine how many sets you want to do over the course of the performance.

My personal favorite, and what I would recommend to any new band, would be to do four sets over the course of the evening. The first one should go for about an hour total, and the next three should go for about 45 minutes each. This gives you over three hours of actual stage time. Add in about 45 minutes for breaks, and you will be all set. This is supposing you put 15 songs in the first set, and 12 in each of the following sets. In order to get to these numbers, you will need to have about 51 songs all together if each one is about an average of three minutes. Once you factor in the adrenaline issue most bands face (playing much faster than you do in practice once you get in front of a crowd), you will need more songs than that.

I think a pretty good number to start out with is probably somewhere around 60 tunes. This is a good number for several reasons. First of all, if you play at the correct speed all night, you will end up with more songs than you need. This will enable you to have a selection so you can substitute in the ones that you are more comfortable with, while avoiding playing the ones that maybe aren't quite ready. Additionally, the more songs you have in your arsenal the better. When you get to the point where you ask the audience for requests, you will be more likely to have what they are looking for, or maybe at least something by one of their favourite artists.

In order to choose songs that will go over well, you are going to have to know your target audience. If you are playing classic rock, you will probably want to play hit songs by The Who, The Beatles or Pink Floyd. Country acts will want to make sure there is plenty of Garth Brooks, Lynyrd Skynyrd and Brad Paisley to please the audience. Taking time to consider your set list might be the most important point I make in this entire book. Believe it or not, this is where a ton of bands get caught up, and later they can't figure out why they are failing to establish a good following.

The problem ultimately starts when the band decides they want to play what they want to play, and not what the audience wants to hear. Take me for example. I am a huge fan of The Smiths. If someone were to ask me what my favourite album of theirs was, I probably wouldn't be able to tell them since I celebrate their entire catalogue. Now, there are some really big hits out there by The Smith's, but I also happen to like some of the lesser know and more bizarre stuff. Even though I want to enjoy what I play, I have to be careful not to fill up the entire set list with things that only I want to hear.

The best example of this I can give comes from the movie Joe Dirt. If you have never seen the film, I highly recommend looking it up. Check out my YouTube page at www.youtube.com/imageten and click on my favorite videos to view the short clip I'm about to describe. No really, look it up so the lesson sticks in your mind. I'm not going to do very much justice to it here, and trust me, David Spade does it much better.

Anyway, the scene I am talking about is when the main character Joe comes upon a fireworks stand. Joe sees that there are snakes and sparklers for sale, but notices a distinct lack of all the cool stuff one would normally find available at such an establishment. Things like Cherry Bombs, Church Burners, Honkey Lighters and Kiddie Chasers (with or without the scooter stick). He asks the owner of this stand where all the "good stuff" is. The owner is confused and says he sells the good stuff. "Snakes and sparklers are all I like", he says. "Well that's your problem," Joe replies, "It's not what YOU like, it's the consumer!" Do yourself a favor and take this lesson to heart early on. Playing music you love while making a living doing it is wonderful. Just don't forget the second part of the equation, and who is playing for the ticket to get in and see your shows.

A Word on Structure

The first set of the night should probably be your strongest and the fastest moving. It should be filled with popular hits that really grab the crowd's attention and fit together well. This is not a set where you want to try experimental stuff or add in tunes that you are a little shaky on. Starting out with your good stuff also means that if something happens and you need more songs, you can always use these ones again at the end of the third or somewhere in fourth set. Keep in mind that you should never plan on recycling songs, but sometimes things happen.

Another great rule of thumb is to always start out with the same song every night. Mainly, you will want to do this because you will know exactly what it should sound like. This can be especially useful for bands who cannot afford to, or do not wish to pay for a professional sound technician (we will discuss this choice later on in the book). If there are any problems, you will be able to notice immediately and fix them before you get the show underway. Think of it as a sound check song, really. In many bands that I have played with, we often used the sound check song as the opening number for this very reason.

When you are piecing your set lists together, don't forget to add a good mixture of songs. Were not talking about genre here, but more about speed and situational songs. During certain points in the evening, you might want to slow things down a bit and invite the couples up to the dance floor. Slow songs are always a good way to get people comfortable with getting out of their seats, which venue owners really like to see. At the conclusion of a slow song, try and throw a dance number in since people are already up. Mix, match and experiment to find out what works for you, but don't forget to throw the slow ones in. I know a lot of slow songs are over played and as a musician you never want to hear them again, let alone play them, but you have to give people what they want.

This leads us into another dreaded territory: crowd participation songs. From the standpoint of a working musician, these can be especially heinous and miserable to play. Songs in this category may include something like "Fins" by Jimmy Buffett where there is a dance or hand motions that go along with the music. Songs in which the audience takes over the vocals like "Friends in Low Places", "Sweet Caroline" or "I Want You to Want Me" also fall into this category. These are just a few examples, but if you have ever played in public for more than an hour, you already know the power these hold. Spread them throughout the evening, and use them wisely.

"But I REALLY Hate That Song!"

While discussing the set list with your band, there are probably going to be songs that come up which people absolutely don't want to play, and that's ok. The problem with this is that these songs are usually the immensely popular ones. For me (and everyone else) those songs have always been "Sweet Home Alabama" and "Freebird". Now, these are both very good songs, and I don't necessarily mind hearing them, but I really, really don't want to play them anymore. Well, if you are adamant that there are things you simply won't play, there is a solution.

When someone would come up to the stage and ask us to play "Sweet Home", we would respond by saying that while we don't know that one (it's always better to say **don't know** rather than **don't play**. It's less condescending), we DO know "Saturday Night Special" by Lynyrd Skynyrd, and we would gladly play that one for him instead. What I'm saying here is that you need to have a backup plan in place for popular songs that you know people are going to ask for, but you simply do not, under any circumstances want to play. For the particular band I'm referencing that never played "Sweet Home", we never had any issues, and people were always very happy to hear other songs. But, that was the only one we refused to play. Try your best to keep the "will not play" number as low as possible, and to remember "the consumer".

What's In a Name?

I thought I would take a few lines here and talk about the all-important "band name". Sadly, this is often times the aspect of creating a band that people put the most time and effort into, because for some reason or another, they deem it as the most important. The fact is though, you can have the most clever name in the world...even one that really says a lot about you, or cleverly depicts and satirizes a nation of cathode junkies, selling their imaginations for quick-fix media hits from the Blockbuster syringe. It will all be for nothing though, unless you are actually able to play and play well. Wasting too much time sitting around thinking about a name is like putting the cart before the horse. If the music is good, trust me, people will come to the show regardless of the name of the band.

When you do get to the point where a name becomes an issue, don't try to think too much into it. I'm not going to go into all the different ways that popular bands got their names (although some of the stories are pretty entertaining), but if you need some inspiration, look up how some of them did it. These stories are usually pretty easy to find on the Internet, and I would be surprised if you didn't know a few of the more popular ones already.

One thing you should probably keep in mind though is that, often times, the best names are the simplest ones. First of all, they are easy for people to remember when they go and tell their friends about the great band they saw last night (think The Who, Green Day or Pink Floyd here). Secondly, you are probably going to want to have a website, Facebook page or other social media stuff up eventually. You want to make it as easy as possible for people to look you up, and trying to spell out some bizarre words that came to you one night in a dream isn't going to make that process any easier for them. Be creative, but keep it reasonable.

Putting It All Together: Practice vs. Rehearsal

With your band members chosen and your songs picked out, you will want to move on to practicing and rehearsing as soon as possible. Before you venture out into playing full shows, you need to ensure that your entire night is down as solid as possible. This is going to require many hours of dedication and practice on your parts, which should pretty much go without saying.

The most important thing you can remember when you get to this point is that there is a distinct difference between "practice" and "rehearsal". Over the years, this has annoyed me so much that I hesitate to even use the word practice when I am talking about more than one person. Practice is something that you do on your own time at home to learn the songs, and rehearsal is something that you do as a group to put all the parts together and polish everything up. For so many bands, too much time is wasted with people coming to rehearsal expecting to learn the songs there. If you go this route, you are costing yourself precious time that you could actually be using to play out.

With this being the case, my recommendation is that everyone in the group takes home a copy of the set list, and using either a CD or YouTube, actually learn their parts on their own. When everyone is ready, get together and go over everything as a group. Ideally, this process should be divided over about four full band rehearsals, with each one representing one fourth of the entire set list. If this is too much, divide that in half and make it into eight sessions. If everyone learns the songs the way they are on the actual track, there should be no need to get together any more than eight times to learn an entire show.

When you actually have everyone together, you should be working on how you plan on stopping and starting each song. You should try to be creative here so not all of your endings sound the same. It works out great when you can just use the endings that are in the recorded versions of the songs, but many times this isn't really possible due to fade outs and such, and you will need to come up with something on your own. Ending everything with drum fills and a stinger looses its cool factor after about five songs, so it's best to try and incorporate some variety here.

Rehearsals also provide a great opportunity for the band to put songs together to create mixes and customizations that can give a unique vibe to your show. An example might be something like a dance band putting together a medley of several songs that work well together. One band I was in combined "Play That Funky Music" and "Superstition", and it turned out to be a huge hit with our crowds. These are both essentially the same song, so it worked. There are a ton of songs that work well together, and all you need to do it sit down and find them. Doing things like this is a great way to keep the audience on the dance floor and involved with the show without a break in the action.

In addition to learning all the music, the singer or singers will also need to be learning the lyrics during this time, which means double the work for them. Over the years, I have never had any problems memorizing lyrics, even when I wasn't the lead signer of a group. The secret? Pick songs that you are familiar with, and listen to a lot of music. The lead singer of the group should be someone to whom this comes naturally. If not, they are going to facing the very daunting task of learning the words to sixty plus songs. As you can imagine, this is a lot easier if you pretty much already know the stuff going in.

Another way to approach this huge learning curve is by carrying the songs around with you wherever you go. In my opinion, the best place to learn music, especially the vocal parts, is in the car on the way to your day job. If you think about it, you are pretty much trapped in there without many entertainment options. Get yourself a half decent sound system, an iPod or a burned CD, and keep listening to the stuff until it sinks in. Once you think you have a part down, turn the stereo off and try to sign a-cappella to really test yourself. Go ahead, no one's listening and if people look at you funny, just look at them like they are the ones with the problem. As another alternative, there are many karaoke tracks available on YouTube that you can look up. Try singing along with these at home.

However you have to do it, memorization is absolutely essential. Let's face it. There are tons of ways that you can make yourself look like an ass on stage. We have all seen this stuff. But really, there is no better (or worse maybe?) way to do this than to go up there with a music stand and sixty sheets of internet-printed song lyrics that are probably wrong anyway. If you really want to look bad, put them all in those little plastic sleeves and make yourself a nice binder with a cover that says "Songs" or something on it. This is incredible tacky, and just screams to the audience of how lazy you are. These people paid money to get in here to see you, and you couldn't even be bothered to learn the material. Half of them could probably get up there and read off a paper into a microphone, so don't plan on impressing anyone. Can you tell I have played with people who have done this before?

A huge part of your success as a band is going to depend on how people perceive you as a professional group. You might just be getting started and still trying to find your way around in the dark, but there are certain things you can do to give yourself the best chance possible for a positive impression. As with many things in life, a lot of this stuff isn't necessarily knowing what to do, but knowing what NOT to do. Reading song lyrics from a lyric sheet is a great example of what not to do, and it's something that can be totally avoided from the beginning by practicing and being prepared.

Part III. - Gear Talk: What To Buy

Get a second hand guitar, chances are you'll go far
If you get in with the right bunch of fellows...

Bachman Turner Overdrive - 1973

What You Need

It's no secret that in order to start a band, you are going to need lots of equipment. Every individual member of the band should have their own instrument, but there are many others pieces of gear that you will need to get out and play while sounding as good as possible. You will have to determine what to get, who is paying for it, and how you are going to get all this stuff back and forth from gig to gig. Additionally, someone is going to actually have to learn how to run this stuff and how to make it sound GOOD. Anyone can learn to hook everything up, but knowing how to make it sound right is a whole different ballgame.

It's also important to note that when you start looking around for this stuff, you are going to be surprised at how expensive some of it can be; especially if you are a first time buyer. You will notice several inexpensive options that can be very tempting if you are on a budget. Forget about them. While it's acceptable to start out with mid-range gear, getting the really low-end cheap stuff will cause nothing but trouble in the long run. It will likely sound terrible and fall apart quickly. Transporting equipment back and forth to shows and practices takes a heavy toll on it, so you are going to want to make sure that whatever you buy can stand up to these conditions.

Something else to strongly consider is who will be paying for all this stuff. A lot of bands decide that they are all going to chip in and buy everything together. This seems like a good idea at first, but can prove to be a mistake when everyone starts fighting and the band decides to break up. What do you do with it now? In a situation like this, you will most likely have to sell everything and split up the money...probably quickly, so you will get much less than you paid for it.

A better idea is to have one person buy the stuff if someone in your group has the means to do it. That way if something happens, there are no issues about deciding who gets what or what gets sold. A better option still is to take someone into the band who already has this stuff to begin with. Generally, these people aren't too difficult to find. When you are trying people out, you might want to give extra points to someone who has a full PA system even though he's no Carlos Santana.

If you do decide to buy a PA system or other band equipment together as a group, another easy way to deal with a breakup is to buy each other out. This should be a pretty simple process as long as everyone agrees on the idea ahead of time. If someone exits the band for whatever reason, the rest of the group just pays that person back for his share of the equipment and that's the end of it. Be sure to save all your receipts so there are no debates about the original cost. From that point on, you can have other people who join the band in the future "buy in", or just consider the stuff paid for. The choice is yours.

Individual Pieces

The truth is, selecting a sound system is a very personal thing. The system you choose will be based on the size of the area you are playing in, how many people will be there, whether it's indoors or outdoors, and what exactly you are running through the system. Are you just using it for vocals, or are you going to run all the instruments through it and use your individual amplifiers as monitors? Sitting here writing this, I cannot know your individual situation and where exactly you intend to be playing. The best thing you can do is find a music store with sales people you can trust, that will listen to your individual needs and come up with something specific.

What I can help you do though, is to get an idea of the different components you will be looking for so that you don't go into the situation totally blind. This way, you will have a good idea of exactly what you need so you don't have to worry about the guy behind the counter trying to sell you a whole bunch of useless crap you don't need because he works on commission.

Speakers

So what are the main components of a startup PA system? You will definitely need two speakers, which are usually referred to as "mains". For an average bar room or show space with a crowd of up to a couple hundred people, two 15" speakers will do the job. You can always add more if you want to. Some good brands to consider in the mid range are Carvin or Peavey. On the upper, you may want to consider JBL, Mackie or Electro Voice (EV). Try to get the ones that are covered in carpeting rather than vinyl. They sound better and stand up to travel a lot better too. Most bands opt for "passive" speakers instead of "active" ones. Active being a speaker that powers itself, and passive being one that needs a power amplifier to make it work.

Power Amplifier (Power Amp or Head Unit)

If you do decide to go with the passive speakers, you are going to need to buy a power amplifier. Some brands to consider might be Sunn, QSC, or Crown if you can afford it. The wattage you decide on will depend on the factors that I listed above. Explain your needs to a sound professional and they will steer you in the right direction. These are delicate pieces of equipment, so you will want to strongly consider having your power amp mounted in a road or rack case. This will enable you to transport it from gig to gig without worry of damage, and will protect it when beer starts spilling all over everything. A case might not be cheap, but it will pay for itself many times over with the amount of money it saves you on costly repairs.

Also, you are going to want to make sure that the speakers can handle the amount of power that's being put out by the amp. If you give them more power than they are rated for, you will blow them up. Blowing up speakers isn't nearly as cool as it sounds, and they can be expensive to have repaired. It's also important to make sure that you are using your speakers to their fullest potential, but at least using too little power won't destroy anything.

Soundboard

In order to plug your instruments into the system and control volume and tone, you are going to need a soundboard. You might also hear these referred to as a "mixing board" or "mixer". You can think about this like the remote control for your television; no matter how many amazing functions your TV has, you aren't going to be able to do much with it without the controls. You will want to find a good quality board; preferably with some sort of warranty. Some quality brands to consider might be Mackie, Peavey or Yamaha.

One of the biggest things you should look for in a soundboard, besides overall quality, is the number of channels that it has. You will need one channel for each microphone you will be using, and preferably more than that. Something could always happen to one of the channels and you may need a backup. You will also need more if you plan on running all of your instruments through the system instead of just the vocals. Always err on the side of caution and remember that it's always better to have too many channels than not enough.

Soundboards should also be equipped with basic features such as reverb. Make certain that the unit you are purchasing has a good reverb on it, as you will need it to make sure that your vocals sound like music and not just someone yelling through a megaphone. If you are buying used, make sure to test this feature out, or at least ask about it. I have had more than one system over the years that I bought and then found out the reverb function was broken. In both of my situations, these came brand new and directly from the factory. If you have a warranty, repairs in an instance like this will be free, but they still take a lot of time to complete. So if possible, it's always best to try it before you buy it.

Combination Soundboard and Power Amp

I think that it's important to mention here that it is possible to buy a soundboard that has a built in power amp, and that it certainly is an option. In my opinion, it's probably best to avoid this route. The main reason for this is that it's sort of the equivalent of putting all of your eggs in one basket; if the thing breaks, you are out two pieces of gear, and instead of just having to replace one piece, you now need to find both. Also, having fewer functions on a single piece of equipment will often make it less likely to break since it's not as complicated. Additionally, you will have greater freedom when it comes to customizing your setup. You can get exactly what you need with each piece without the need to compromise on one or the other.

One final note on soundboards. Just like the power amp, you are going to want to get something to protect this thing, as it is a fragile piece of equipment. Not only are flying drinks or an accidental drop your enemy, but you also have to watch out for dust. Over time, dust can accumulate inside the individual sliders and cause a channel to have an awful noise or stop functioning entirely. This is another reason to have more channels than you think you will need. A nice case will keep the board functioning and also make sure all the buttons and knobs stay attached. If you are keeping the board out of the case for any length of time (such as while it is set up in a practice space), make sure to cover it with a towel to keep it clean. Soundboard repair is costly, but luckily it's almost entirely avoidable through proper care and maintenance.

Monitors

Another essential PA system component are the monitors. These are smaller speakers that sit on the floor and face upward towards the musicians. These let you hear what's coming out of the mains so you know what you sound like and can hear all the other instruments. Do not even attempt to play a show without monitors. You will be surprised at how difficult it will be to hear individual parts once everyone starts playing and the audience starts screaming. If the person mixing your sound knows what they're doing, they will be able to give each musician a custom mix. The bass player, for example, might need to hear the drummer louder than anything else, so he will have the drums turned up the loudest in his mix, and so on.

Ideally, each musician should have their own monitor. In a smaller space though, it's possible to have one or more people share as long as they can agree on the mix. You will definitely want to be sure that every person who is singing has their own individual monitor. If the lead singer can't hear himself, he will have no idea whether he is off pitch or not. By the same token, the people trying to do harmonies or background vocals will have nothing to go off of if they can't hear the lead singer. Buy enough monitors to cover all these situations and plan ahead.

Just like the PA speakers, you can get these active or passive. If you are running a lower wattage power amp, you will probably want to strongly consider purchasing active monitors. This will allow the power to be flowing to more essential areas like your main speakers, which are of course what your audience will be hearing. A higher wattage power amp is going to cost more money, but active monitors or other speakers will also cost more money too. One way or another, you are going to be paying for the power.

If I had to choose between one or the other, I would say the best route would be to just buy a more powerful power amp and go with passive speakers all around. As we mentioned before, even the most rugged equipment is fragile and can break. Passive speakers are a lot less likely to have things go wrong with them, and they are also lighter weight. A high quality power amp that has been well maintained will also hold it's value much better in the long run than the finest powered speakers, so spending the extra money here is probably the better investment.

Ear Monitors

If you have a lot of money burning a hole in your pocket, you can also choose to go with an "ear monitor" system. These things are just what they sound like - monitors that fit inside your ear. They look almost exactly like a hearing aid, and they are much easier to store and transport than conventional monitors. While you may want to consider upgrading to these at some point, I would recommend going with the normal ones to start out with. Even though they are bigger and heavier, they are less expensive and way less of a hassle to use.

Microphones

Obviously, microphones are another vital piece of equipment for the working musician. There are several different kinds of mics, and they all have their individual purposes. Some are used primarily for vocals, while others are intended for use in amplifying instruments such as an acoustic guitar or drums. The microphones you choose will mainly depend on the specific functions you want them to serve.

Wired or Wireless?

So here's the big question. Should you be using wireless microphones or not? What about headset mics? Are those a good idea? For the most part, the answer to these questions is a resounding "NO". Wireless microphones will never sound as good as corded ones, and unless you are Britney Spears or a motivational speaker, you will look like an ass if you try to get away with wearing one.

Unless we are talking about the most expensive wireless microphones available (and even those sometimes), the difference in sound quality will be apparent to anyone who possesses a working pair of ears. Trust me, you do not have to have a degree in sound engineering to hear how awful these things sound. On top of the horrible interference and other offensive noises, you will have to worry about range, batteries, any other electronic equipment that's operating in the area, and finding a space to put the receiver. Needless to say, wireless microphones are also significantly more fragile than the regular corded variety. By using one, you are increasing you chances of having something go wrong.

One exception to this might be if you have a dedicated singer who is not playing an instrument. This guy will probably want to find as many ways as possible to look busy, and walking all over the stage or being able to go into the audience to dance around might fill some of his time. If you consider some classic examples from professional musicians though, you will find that most didn't seem to have any problem functioning with a regular mic. Take Roger Daltrey for example. He had no problem staying busy and being entertaining with a corded microphone, and even made swinging it around part of his act. If it's good enough for him, it's probably good enough for you, too.

When it's all said and done, the most important thing to consider in this debate is the overall quality of sound produced by each type of microphone. Ask any working musician, and more than nine times out of ten, they will tell you that a good microphone with a high quality cord is the way to go. As you will often times find with all different types of musical equipment, the latest technology and newest stuff on the shelf is rarely the path to the best sound. People play vintage instruments and hoard old gear for a reason. Listen for the difference yourself, and I think you will agree.

Types of Microphones

There are several different companies out there that make high quality vocal mics. Some of them are Sennheiser, Electro Voice and AKG to name just a few. In my opinion though, Shure makes the best microphones you can get for the money. Their audio gear has been the industry standard over the years for use in both live and recorded music. No matter what you are looking for, you can't go wrong if you stick with them. I have listed a few of the most popular models to help get you started in your search. If you buy several of each, you can mic up an entire band and sound great.

Shure SM58 - For a vocal mic, the SM58 is fantastic. They are inexpensive, and almost always in stock at any decent music store. Outfit your lead and background vocalists with these and you will be in good shape. Every 58 that I have ever owned has been dropped hundreds of times and banged around during travel, but they still work great. In a pinch, they can also be used as instrument mics as well.

Shure SM57 - This is probably the most versatile microphone on the planet. It can be used for vocals, but is primarily used for miking instruments. Try one on your acoustic guitars and on the drums...especially for a snare and hi hat. The SM57 is very small and much like it's SM58 cousin, it's built to take a beating and is virtually indestructible. If you get a few of these, you can plan on putting them in your will.

Drum Mics

A lot of bar bands tend to overlook putting mics on the drums, thinking they are loud enough on their own. As a drummer and connoisseur of fine sound, I believe this is a terrible mistake. The main point of miking drums is not to make them louder, but to adjust the tone and make them a part of the overall mix. All too often, live bands have a sound that isn't very cohesive and sounds like separate people playing at once instead of one single song that flows. Adding the drums to the mix with microphones is a great way to prevent this.

If you have someone who knows what they are doing mixing the sound, they can mix the drums to where they turn into something you feel rather than just the random noise of someone banging on something. You know that feeling in your chest when someone hits a bass drum? That's what you should be going for.

In order to do this, you will need to invest in some mics made especially for drums. SM57's all around would work for every drum except the bass, but having actual drum mics will be easier to deal with. This is mainly due to the fact that they come with clips that are specially made for attaching to the rim of the drum, and they are the appropriate size. You should definitely be using a 57 on the snare and hi-hat, but go with dedicated drum mics for everything else.

It might be a good idea to start with a drum mic kit that will have everything you need in all in one. Once again, Shure makes some great kits that would most likely fit your needs and give you the most bang for your buck. Most of these will come with PG56's for use on the toms, and a PG52 for the bass drum. Even if you decide that drum mics are not a priority right now, you will still want to make sure to at least mic the snare and hi-hat and bass drum. As you begin to add more gear to your arsenal, you may also want to consider picking up a few condensers to use as overhead mics for the drums. These will pick up the cymbals and other ambient sounds, making for a smoother and fuller overall tone.

One Final Note on Drum Miking

If you intend to mic all of the drums (and you should), there are steps that you can take to avoid using up all the channels on your main mixing board. As a drummer, I firmly believe that drums almost always sound their best when properly miked, and that this should be done whenever possible. Drum mics are not meant to amplify sound as much as they are meant to provide the ability to fine tune their tone and make them a part of the mix. The problem is that the average drummer will probably have at least five drums, and want at least one overhead condenser for cymbals and ambient noise. That would equal six channels on your main board, which could leave you running out of space.

A better option in this situation is to make sure that the drummer has his own, smaller board to plug into. From there, the drums can be individually mixed, and then that board can be connected to the main board. Since you've already gotten the levels on the drummer's board, all you really need to worry about now is volume. The best part is that you have only used a single channel on the main board, and will be able to keep things less cluttered.

For a secondary board like this, it's important to look for one with "phantom power". This will allow the board to turn on, function and send a signal without the use of a power amp. This power won't be enough to run a whole band off of, but it will work for what you need it to just by plugging it into any electrical outlet.

Cords

Wow, talk about something that sounds basic. Putting a section in this book on cords might seem like the equivalent of someone asking you to check that your computer is plugged in before you decide that it's broken. I assure you there is more to it than that. Plus, sometimes people really do forget to plug the computer in. The point being, if your setup isn't sounding quite right but everything seems to be in order, it might be time to check the quality of your cords. We're mainly talking about things like PA and mic cords here, but this also applies to instrument cables. Why buy a quality piece of high dollar equipment and then hook it up with the cheapest cable you can find?

The debate about whether or not people can hear the difference between one brand of cable over another continues to rage on. Discussing that particular aspect is probably beyond the scope of this book, and depends largely on your personal listening experiences. What I will tell you is that the quality of cables varies widely from manufacturer to manufacturer. So, while this may not necessarily mean you can hear highs or lows better, it does mean that you will hear a difference once the thing stops working, falls apart, or frays and electrocutes someone. Cords are one item that no one ever seems to have enough of, so you want to make sure to buy quality in the first place and take care of the ones you have.

Every online music store (and some larger big box stores) has their own brand of cords that are generally quite a bit cheaper than name brands. Often times, the quality of these can be pretty subpar. Going for at least a middle of the road quality brand will save a lot of aggravation and wasted money. Check the reviews, and if at all possible, get something that has a warranty!

Some Final Tips on Cords and Cables

- Buy some colored electrical tape and put a strip around each end of an XLR cable or other cord to know whose is whose and what goes where. In bands that use the same general setup all the time, you will pretty much know how long everyone's cables have to be, and some may have different general preferences on brand/quality etc. Color-coding will help speed things up, and keep stage clutter to a minimum.

- In order to make your cords last longer, you will want to make sure you are storing them correctly. To do this, you should wind the cord between the thumb and first finger and around the elbow. Most importantly, use the opposite hand to twist the cord in its "natural direction". This will help prevent the cord from shorting out, and will greatly increase its overall life.

- Carry (The Handyman's Secret Weapon) Duct Tape: Tape as many cords as you can to the floor. We're mainly talking about ones that will not be moving for the duration of the performance, such as those for instrument mics or the PA system. This will prevent personal injuries and damage done to gear from having cables and wires torn out.

Lighting

No matter where you are playing, unless it's an outdoor venue during the day, things are likely to be dark. Bars, private parties and clubs, and even the biggest concert halls tend to keep the lights turned down as low as possible. As you probably know, "last call" in a bar is usually associated with the lights going all the way up, and people scattering like roaches. So how are you supposed to be seen in all of this darkness? With stage lighting, of course.

Some of the venues you play will provide a stage with some basic lighting, and some might even have some cool state of the art stuff. If you are like the average band though, you will more often than not be finding yourselves working in less than ideal conditions; maybe the corner of a dance floor or on the back of parked trailer in the middle of a corn field. Hey, it happens. In these situations, you are going to need to provide your own lighting.

To do this, you have several different options. As with sound systems, you could of course bring someone in to do it professionally, but this really isn't necessary. Unless you are playing an early Pink Floyd tribute show, the lighting is there to make the band easier to see rather than to be entertaining. If a dance floor or the like needs lighting for the audience, leave your disco ball at home. That kind of thing is up to the venue. You should only be concerned with the very basics.

The most straightforward approach is to buy a couple racks of lights that are referred to as "wash lighting". These are generally sold to DJ's and come with a stand, lighting bar, and 4 different colored lights. The most economical set of these are a line made by Chauvet called the CoreBar. These sets are reasonably well made, come with a carrying case and definitely get the job done. Some specific models can even be programmed to have the lights flash in a specific pattern or along with the music. Buy two sets of these, place them up on both sides of the band, and you are pretty much all set.

These small set-ups are just a starting point, and you can go as crazy as you want with this stuff. Tons of bands develop a cool and unique look by employing strobe lighting, fog machines, spotlights and other effects. The possibilities are almost endless. As previously mentioned, nearly all of this stuff can be found in the DJ section of music stores. Having appropriate lighting for the venues in which you play not only looks professional, but also can be added in as a selling point when negotiating gigs. Managers like to hear that you are coming equipped with everything you need for the performance so they don't have anything to worry about besides getting people in the door.

Other Miscellaneous Items:

These would be things like mic stands, mic clips, speaker stands, batteries, drum rugs, road cases etc. Generally, just follow the same thought processes listed above when buying these things and you will be fine. There will be other items that as you go along, you will find out that you need. Take note of these and try to be prepared for any eventuality. Plan ahead, and remember...buy cheap, buy twice.

Part IV. - Selling Yourself

I play the big show rooms in Vegas!
I need this place like I need a shotgun blast to the face!

Tony Clifton - (Man on the Moon, 1999)

Advertising

At this point, you should have your band members, your set lists and your gear all ready to go. You have been practicing on your own time, gotten together for rehearsals, and everything sounds great. Now what do you do with all of this? Since people probably aren't just going to knock on your door looking for you, you are going to have to go looking for them. Before we can actually get to that step though, there is even more additional groundwork to be laid. I know all of this stuff sounds like a lot of work, but it will pay off in the end.

Early on in the life of your band, most of the shows you get will be the result of seeking out your own venues and booking them. In order to do this properly, you are going to need some material that you can put into peoples hands to help them get a feel for whether or not your group is the right fit for their specific venue, party etc. This will be through the use of web presence as well as some sort of physical promotional kit. How much of each of these you use will be mostly dependent on the types of places you are looking to play.

If, for example, you are looking to play the hottest new club or at some college frat parties, a Facebook group, YouTube videos or an account on Reverbnation will probably be the only things you need. If you are looking to play at the local bar, a Moose Club event or a high-end function, you might want to make sure you are able to sell yourself with a physical kit. While I have played shows of both these styles, the discussion here is mainly geared toward the latter, as I find it's where the most money is to be made.

While you may occasionally find a bar or nightclub with a nice website where you can submit your information, you will more often than not need to go to these places in person. The best time to do this is generally during the middle of the day when not a lot is going on at the venue. You will often times find the owner sitting at the bar, chain smoking cigarettes and watching The Price is Right at about 2 PM. This is probably the best time for your approach.

Most of the time, these people have a ton of different bands lined up that have been playing these spots for years, so you will want to make it as easy as possible for them to hear your stuff and give you a chance. Not to sound too judgmental, but if some of these people even own a computer, they still probably won't be bothered enough to remember your information and go look it up online. Remember, we want to make it as easy and pleasant an experience as possible for venue owners to book our shows.

So, what will you need to make this happen? Enter the demo tape...

Making a Demo

Even though they are still often referred to as a "tape", these things are usually found on CD now a' days. Somehow, an actual cassette tape does not exactly scream "quality" if you know what I mean. CD's are still a great way of passing out your demos since we have reached a period in time where even the most elderly bar and club owners understand them, but they aren't so old fashioned that they are totally obsolete. Generally, any bar will probably have a CD player sitting around somewhere, so the person you are giving the demo to can put it right on and listen to it. If they don't have a CD player, you might want to reconsider that particular venue.

A CD also has some basic advantages over handing someone a piece of paper with a web address on it. First, it is an actual, physical item that people can handle. This makes somebody think twice before tossing it in the trash or sticking it in a pocket and forgetting about it. Subconsciously, it also suggests that you took the time to actually make something physical and put money into it, so it must be worth at least something. As musicians, we all know this isn't really any different than having an MP3 or other type of recording, but the general public doesn't think that way.

How easy is it to turn on your iPhone and make a recording? Anybody can do that. Putting information, let alone a quality recording on a CD, is something that was never really understood by the general public. It wasn't like during the tape recorder generation when anyone could by a recorder and press the red button. Even to do a bad home recording, you need to have the gear and know how to use it. I really do think people still consider this on some level when you hand them a CD, whether they realize it or not.

Demo Contents

When creating a demo, there are many factors that need to be considered. What songs will you select? How many? What order will you put them in? Will the recordings be from a studio, from live events, or be recorded in somebody's garage on an iPhone or home recording software? Additionally, you will want to think about how you will package this demo. Do you want straight up CD-R's labeled with a Sharpie or will you opt for professional packaging?

Obviously, you will want to select songs which reflect your chosen genre of music and that you play particularly well. If you have decided to take my advice and play cover songs, you will want to give some serious consideration to including these on your demo. You want to give the bar or club manager an accurate representation of what they will be getting when they decide to book your band.

The first issue to consider is whether or not you want to use studio recordings or live ones. Chances are, if you are reading this book, you are just starting out in the business and don't have a whole lot of live shows from which to gather material. Even if you are already out and playing, you have to consider the fact that obtaining listenable live recordings isn't the easiest thing in the world to do; you will need lots of additional equipment and someone who knows what they are doing to take the raw recordings and turn them into something that really showcases your talents. I have taken multiple approaches to this in the past, so read each one over, discuss it with your band, and make your decision.

How Many Songs?

The truth is, most people will not sit down and listen to your entire demo and put an incredible amount of thought into whether they should hire you or not. Chances are, they will listen to a few seconds of each song, decide if you are awful or not, and if you would be a good fit for their usual crowd. If you are decent, a good fit, and present your band as being professional, you will probably have a pretty good chance. With that being said, how many songs should go onto a demo?

Since we already know that people's attention spans are limited, it's obvious that we shouldn't load the things up to capacity with a whole bunch of different stuff. You will want to shoot for something that encompasses what exactly it is that your band does, all within a reasonable amount of time. With this in mind, I have found that the best number of songs for a demo is three. That way, you can showcase a decent variety, have a beginning, middle and end, and still come in at a number that doesn't seem like too much or too little. People *like* the number three.

Whether you decide to do three songs or not, the first song should obviously be your best one. Hopefully it will be something that the buyer recognizes and likes. This is another strength of the cover song. People already know them, and provided that we do them well, they should give nearly as good of a listening experience as hearing the real thing. Maybe Billy the club owner really likes the Beatles, but two of the best ones are dead and he can't afford to get the rest of them to show up. If you do a great cover of "A Day in the Life", your band might be a great consolation prize. Take note though, that Billy will immediately recognize if you leave out the *ohhs and ahhhs* after the part in the middle, and he will be really pissed off that you messed up his favourite song. Do your best, and hopefully this will not be an issue.

The second song on your demo should be one that still fits within your genre, but maybe something that you don't do too much of. A good example of this might be putting a slow dance song in the number two slot. This will show the buyer that even though you can really get the place rocking, you can also slow it down to get some couples up on the dance floor. This is only an example, so make sure you know your own repertoire and use some good judgment here.

The final song out of the three should be something similar to the first track, but by a different artist and maybe with a different feel. Perhaps something that isn't overplayed and that the band actually enjoys playing. Using the classic rock example, you might want to stick the Beatles in at #1, slip "Wonderful Tonight" by Eric Clapton in at #2, and throw in "Going Mobile" by The Who at #3. This selection demonstrates the idea that your set choices will be logical, but contain a nice variety as well.

You do not have to follow this formula exactly. Here is an actual example of a three-track demo that I recorded with a 90's rock band, which varies slightly from the above formula. The important point here is that no matter what you end up doing, make sure you have a good, well thought out reason for doing it. The tracks on this demo were:

I.   Counting Blue Cars by Dishwalla
II. Mr. Jones by Counting Crows
III. In the Meantime by Spacehog

If you are in the market for a 90's band, you have most likely heard "Counting Blue Cars". Even though some people might not know the name or the band, it's one of those tracks that you know for sure you have heard somewhere before. It's also a song that we knew we could play live and have it sound just like the recording without

THE BAR BAND SURVIVAL GUIDE

any issues. As I mentioned before, this is a very important factor.

The second track, "Mr. Jones", is a song that everyone who likes music from the 90's at all is guaranteed to know. Not too many bands will attempt to play it though, due to the fact that it's pretty challenging both instrumentally and vocally. In particular, the song was chosen to highlight the strengths of the individual musicians in the band (who were all quite good) while at the same time showing the buyer that we played some tunes that aren't exactly considered "standards".

The last song, "In The Meantime", was selected mainly because we all liked playing it and it and it was fun to record. At the same time, it certainly fit into our chosen genre, we could duplicate it live, and it is something that would be recognizable (maybe not by name, but definitely by listening) to most fans of the genre. Mostly though, that one was recorded for us.

You will notice that I didn't recommend putting any original songs on your demo. There is a reason for this, even though I mentioned earlier that there is nothing wrong with working a few originals in here and there. Sticking with covers is mainly due to the fact that the buyer is going to be listening to this disc trying to judge whether you are any good or not. Make it easy for them. If

I gave you a CD comprised of Hoomi music (Mongolian throat singing), you might be able to tell me if you liked it or not, but really wouldn't be able to say whether it was good or bad unless you have heard other people play it too. That's because you don't have a frame of reference. You can probably bet that the general population won't want to pay a cover charge and drink 8 dollar rum and Cokes while listening to it though.

Live Recording

When you submit a live recording to a buyer, they really know exactly what they are getting. They can hear the responses of the crowd (or lack thereof) and the front man's level of ability in engaging an audience. The absolute truth is, nearly every band is going to sound different live than they do in the studio. Pretty much anyone with any musical ability whatsoever can be made to sound halfway decent in a proper recording environment with optimal conditions and unlimited retakes. If you have a great crowd response, there's no question that you should want that to reflect on your resume.

One of the drawbacks to this sort of recording is the fact that you will probably want to avoid an all encompassing ambient microphone, since most venues in the world do not have the acoustics of the La Scala opera house. If we could do this, it would be a rather simple affair...set up a microphone in the middle of the room and press record. The ugly truth of the matter is that recordings of this nature often come out sounding like those times when you are stopped at a red light next to someone who is so proud of what they are listening to that they turn it all the way up in order to share it with the rest of us. In other words, it sounds like trash.

Live recordings from both popular and non-popular bands still exist due to the fact that each individual instrument and vocal can be miked, run through the board and then mixed down later to form a listenable song. The crowd can also be miked and mixed in appropriately to reflect the live atmosphere without being too overbearing. Plus, you are able to edit stuff out in case some drunk guy starts incessantly yelling for Freebird. If you have the ability and this is something you are interested in trying, read on to learn about some computer software that can help you make this possible.

If this sounds like too much work, I would be inclined to agree with you. If you are still determined to record live, you can bypass most of the hassle by paying someone else to come in and do it for you. If you want to go in this direction, a sound engineer will come in, set up their equipment and get what they need. These companies will then mix everything down (for an additional cost) and hand you a finished product. Unfortunately, these types of services can be extremely cost prohibitive, especially to new bands that are just getting started.

On top of all that, you also have to keep in mind that you aren't guaranteed to get any listenable/usable material in just one show. Maybe you don't end up playing a song as well as you would have liked to, or maybe no one shows up to the show and things are dead silent. Maybe you end up getting a Blues Brothers style hostile crowd and you never want to think about that show again. Anything could happen, but you are still going to have to pay the sound engineer for their time. This is the reason that many of history's most popular bands have their live albums sourced from several different shows. Don't believe me? Check it out for yourself. Think about it. The odds of you hitting everything you need to in one shot, and doing it well enough that it is up to your standards are pretty slim. Unless of course your standards are really low, which in that case, good luck.

For these reasons, I have always tried to avoid the live recording for use in demos. The process is long and expensive, and the costs can add up quickly. If you do have the ability to live record on your own at an acceptable level of quality, this changes the game a little bit. In this scenario, you would be able to record every single show you do and you are bound to eventually catch lightning in a bottle. If not in one single show, then maybe over many shows. If you need paying gigs right now or would have to pay someone else to do it, however, you might want to consider another option.

Studio Recording

A second option you might want to consider is studio recording. When most people think of going into the studio to lay down tracks, they imagine it costing a huge amount of money and taking up a ton of time. Neither one of these has to be true, provided that you know what you are doing and come into the thing well prepared. A quick search on the Internet will most likely reveal several recording studios in your area, and you just might be surprised at the affordable rates you can get if you shop around.

When working bands consider studio demos, you sometimes hear arguments against them, mainly centering on the fact that they are dishonest representations of the band. This can definitely be true. We have all heard studio recordings that turned out to be nothing like the live product turned out by the band, and almost always in a negative way. If you select this option to record your demo, the key is being able to actually live up to the quality represented on the recording. In other words, don't play a cover of "Hotel California" for your demo where you go back and record all the guitar parts in tracks, then show up at a gig with three people. You can't possibly recreate all of that, so don't go that route. It will make you look bad.

Instead, select songs that you can actually play live, and play well. Additionally, you don't have to go through and record everything in individual tracks over a period of days or weeks. Any good studio should have the ability to do a "live" style recording. Basically, the engineer will set everybody up in different rooms with their own mics to isolate their sound and give the entire band headphones with the overall mix. This way, you can get a great sounding recording without really "cheating". If done in this fashion, the sound is exactly what the buyer can plan on getting before factoring in the environment in which the band will be working. This takes care of the dishonestly argument and should leave you with a recording that was worth your time and money.

As far as studio pricing is concerned, much of it is very affordable, especially when you consider the fact that it will probably be split up between several band mates. The studio I have used exclusively over the past few years is excellent and charges 50.00 an hour for recording and mixing. This is a pretty great price considering the quality you will get and the headaches you will save. As long as you come in prepared, you should end up with a product that will pay major dividends when it comes time to book your shows.

This brings us to another important point. Be ready to go into the studio. I have actually ended up in a recording session with people who were not confident with their parts and thought that they would figure out how everything was going to go together when they arrived. The clock is ticking and this is absolutely the wrong way to approach things. Come into the studio confident that you know your parts, and it will take you literally one or two takes per song to have everything down, assuming you are going with a live style recoding option rather than a more precise and drawn out process.

Some studios will charge you for loading, unloading and setup times, while others will not. This is a great question to ask before you decide on a studio in which to record your demo. As far as timing, you should expect about 1 hour for each song that you will record (provided you know the material) and about 1 hour per song for the engineer to do the mixing. If you can find a place that has a 50.00 per hour rate, you are looking at about 300.00 total (400 if they charge for setup and breakdown) for a quality demo, which should land a ton of shows for you. In my personal opinion, you can't beat this option.

One last tip for studio recording is to select a sound engineer that you like and stick with them. Not only for demos or other recordings that you might do in the future, but also for the mixing process after the recording is complete. The guy who actually took the recording will already have an idea of what he wants to do with it, and will have a better feel for the band than someone coming in cold. Keeping the same guy will also save you money in the long run since he will already know what he's working with.

When your project is wrapped up at the recording studio, you will most likely be handed a blank CD-R in a paper envelope. From this point, what you do with it is up to you. The studio should have the capability to run you off a number or copies of the disc, but this probably isn't worth the added expense since it can easily be done at home on any computer that's been built in the last 15 years. You can choose to have the CD replicated instead of duplicated (a service the studio is likely to offer - the cost is higher, but the sound quality will be better), but this is almost certainly not worth the added cost. Unless you want fancy packaging, take the thing home and burn it yourself.

Home Recording

One final option we will consider is recording your demo at home. This sort of combines elements from the studio and live recording settings. You have some control over your environment and are able to stop and start over again at will, but you won't likely have all the luxuries of the studio available such as isolation booths, professional engineers etc. If you already have the training and some equipment sitting around, this might even be able to save you some money. For do-it-yourselfers on a budget, you will be happy to know that there are some free resources out there on the Internet to help you along the way.

Proper equipment for home recording studio is expensive. Going over every piece of gear you will need for such an undertaking is beyond the scope of this book. If you need a comprehensive list of these things, this is a pretty good sign that you probably aren't ready to jump into something like this just yet, and turning to a professional is most likely your best option. In addition to the expense, you also have to factor in the time it will take you to accomplish your goal. Something that might take 6 hours of studio time could wind up taking weeks, and leave you with a product that still doesn't sound right.

Home recording studio used to record my full-length album Industrial Refuse

If you are not too experienced, but have the gear (or the money to buy it) and the time to learn, there are a few places you can turn to for help. The most obvious one would be YouTube. There are various lessons from all sorts of people with different experience levels posted there that you can refer to. Otherwise, I would recommend checking out the forums at homerecording.com where you can read advice from others and ask questions.

If you have your recording gear but don't want to shell out a ton of money on recording software, there are lots of options available. The most commonly used software in professional recording studios would be Pro Tools by Avid, which can cost 700.00 or more. A more inexpensive alternative that I can personally recommend would be Mixcraft by Acoustica. At 74.95, it's pretty hard to beat the quality of this software. It's an easy interface to learn, and you will definitely get your money's worth if you put in the time to acquaint yourself with the different features it offers.

If you are on an extremely low budget and need recording software, there are still other options. There are several programs out there, but the only one I can personally recommend is called Audacity. This software is open source, and available for free as an online download. It is easy to use, and works well considering the price. I have recorded entire albums using only this software, and they turned out well enough to be downloaded regularly on iTunes and Amazon as well as be accepted by Pandora

Internet radio. There will still be a learning curve here, but anyone with some ambition and a little bit of time should be able to figure this program out without much of a problem. To check out what my band was able to do with this software over 10 years ago, visit our website at notafew.com or listen for free on YouTube or Pandora.

Demo Packaging

Now that you have your demo recorded, you need to decide on how you want to package it. If you have a disc full of cover songs, it probably doesn't make sense to go out and get something fancy made up since it contains other people's material. There are a ton of different web based companies who will print your demo on silver or full color discs, insert them into fancy eco style digi-packs and wrap them up for you for a substantial fee. Before you go out and do this though, consider these few points.

First of all, if your disc contains copyrighted material, you can't sell it without being in violation of the law. With this being the case, fancy and extensive packaging would seem to be a total waste of money. If you want to sell these recordings (and you should *technically* be doing this anyway if you are recording covers), go online and visit the Harry Fox Agency. Getting a license to do this legally is actually very simple and surprisingly affordable. Basically, you pay a flat fee based on the number of units you plan on selling (i.e. the number of CD's you will be printing or the amount of downloads you expect to sell). Doing this might make sense if you end up recording an album of original material later on and decide you want to include a cover song that your band is particularly great at playing.

You should also consider the fact that in the best-case scenario, the buyer who is handed the CD will put it in the stereo, listen to it for a few seconds, hire you and then toss the disc. Unless you are doing something insanely memorable like playing "Thunderstruck" on the water glasses, not many people will hang onto your disc. If they want to hear recorded music, they will probably go with the original artist. LIVE music, on the other hand, is totally different. In these cases, people want the experience of going to a show and interacting with a live band. Right now, we are selling shows, not records. So is a fancy package or disc printing worth it? Probably not.

My best advice would be to check Amazon or NewEgg for deals on a good-looking spindle of CD-R's (use the blank white or silver ones please...otherwise it will look terrible) and buy them by the hundred. Find some white paper sleeves with or without a little plastic window in them, grab a black Sharpie and you are in business. If you really want to get fancy, you can print yourself up some labels and stick them on the disc. This tends to look nice and professional. If you really can't let go of the idea of including a band logo or some other form of cover art, you might want to consider this option. Print out the art work at home, cut it out and then insert the papers into the sleeves to make use of the little window. This will add a touch of professionalism and cost you next to nothing.

If you choose to go with just writing on the disc itself, be sure to include the band name and the telephone number of the person who does your booking. In this case, the person will probably be you. If you want to, it would also be acceptable to add your website address just in case someone wants to see it. Even if they don't look at it, just the fact that they know that you have a website can add to your overall perceived value in the mind of the buyer.

Some examples of demo discs that I've used successfully over the years

Additional Marketing Materials

At this point, you should be all set with your demo and be ready to hand it over to some prospective buyers. Before you go for it, you may want to consider adding some supplemental materials, along with your demo, to create a more substantial promotional packet. This can be as tastefully small or as unnecessarily large as you want it to be. With various online sites that provide quick and inexpensive printing, you could hand out anything from a logo keychain to a wiffleball bat with your face on it if you wanted to. Some items are more reasonable to consider than others, so I will just cover some of the most basic ones.

Business cards are always a good idea, and they can be obtained very inexpensively from some of the online resources that I have listed in the back of this book. Even in the technology driven world we live in today, a nicely designed business card will often be something that is saved by a prospective buyer. Some printers will give you a set of a few hundred for absolutely free. You should be aware though, that these companies will include their name and contact information on the back of these free cards, which makes them look amateurish and just generally awful.

It would probably be better to have no business card at all than to have one that looks bad. Some basic rules to follow are to avoid having too much information, information that makes you sound unprofessional, or hand writing stuff to alter your card. These things are cheap. Buy more instead of scratching things out. Here's an example that breaks all the rules and looks like trash:

None other than "Jake the Snake's" card from Part VI.

When designing your card, keep it simple and professional. The band name, website, phone number and maybe some social media links will be all you need. If you have one, it's not a bad idea to include a slogan here. One of the country bands I played in for years used the slogan "A New Experience in Country Music". This small addition to the card took it from looking too generic to just right. Play around with it for a while and then order some cards. In addition to use in your promotional package, you can give a bunch of these out to every band member, stick them up on community bulletin boards or hire someone to shove them in peoples faces on Las Vegas Boulevard. Lots of options.

Promotional flyers are also inexpensive to design (or free if you have some computer skills) and dirt cheap to copy. Consider designing a single flyer that might contain a photo of your band, quotes or small reviews from past venues, social media and web addresses, contact information etc. and including it with your demo. These are a lot less expensive to have made up than brochures or rack cards and can get the job done.

Reviews and articles you might accumulate about your band that have been printed in newspapers or even online would be something worth printing out and adding to the packet. Potential buyers probably won't sit down and read through all of this stuff, but it does make you look more professional for just having it in there.

Folders can also be a nice option for tying everything together. Online printing sites can whip some up for you with your band name and logo, or you can opt for plain ones that can be found at any stationary store. You might even get lucky and find some at a dollar store, but don't cheap out too much here. Just take whatever you have, stick it in the folder and start knocking on doors.

You will, of course, want to avoid handing these things out to just anybody. That could get expensive pretty quickly. When we get into approaching potential buyers, you will get an idea of who to leave this stuff with and who not to leave it with. Over the years, I have done all of this at one time or another. It all works, but I still feel like I only need a blank, hand labeled CD-R in a white envelope when approaching potential buyers. I don't really think you need the rest of it as long as you are confident and have some idea of how to talk to people. If having a nice presentational packet will make this easier for you in the beginning though, it will be worth it's weight in gold.

Online Presence

Throughout this section, we have been referencing social media and websites quite a bit, but we haven't talked about getting those things started. The fact is, online presence (specifically social media) is huge today, and it will help you get booked, at least on some level. The most important reason to have these things though is to provide a place where you can interact with your fans, have your music heard, and maybe eventually sell your own merchandise.

You will be able to get a basic understanding of what you need to know about an online presence from this book. If you want to go more in depth with social media, however, I recommend picking up a copy of The Social Media Magician by Dan Sperry as a fantastic resource. Although this book was written with magicians in mind, it would be extremely useful to anyone who is seeking to grow their brand online. Dan has become one of the most successful international magic stars on the planet, building his empire through live performances and social media. This should sound familiar, since we are trying to do the exact same thing here with music. It's not really that different. Check the resources section of this book for information on how to order a copy.

Website

One of the most important things anybody who is selling something in the world today can have is a website. This is another one of those things that if you really don't know what you are doing, you should probably come up with the money and pay someone to do it for you. This site is going to serve as your online resume, so it's very important it's done correctly and contains all the information you will need to sell your band.

If you do decide to do it yourself and are a beginner, there are a few resources you can use to make sure you still put out a good product. Many people have had success with using Wordpress templates, which are very user friendly and look pretty good. Wordpress offers a lot of different levels of service, and some are more expensive than others. Some are totally free. Check out their website, sign up for an account and go from there. If you mess around with it for a while and decide taking on the project yourself is doable, this would be a great site to use.

If you are a Mac user, another great option would be to use iWeb. This program comes free with every Mac, and it is very easy to use, even for the beginner. You can use some of the pre-made templates that come with the program for free, or you can buy a custom designed layout from the web. Some of these are 10.00 or less, and I have included a few websites in the resources section of this book where you can find some different template options. After you download the files and open them up in iWeb, you just have to fill in your information and photos. If you were capable of purchasing this book online or downloading it to an e-reader, building a website in this program is certainly within your capabilities.

Another popular company that will let you build your own website is Wix.com This site offers services that are similar to Wordpress, but it seems that people are a lot less satisfied with it. It wouldn't hurt to give them a try since your experiences may be different, but my advice would be to look elsewhere if you can. As with all of these options, it doesn't hurt to look around at reviews online before you get started, and especially before you decide to spend money on a plan. Both Wordpress and Wix will let you try before you commit any money, so keep that in mind.

Whether or not you decide to build your own website or not, your main concentration should be on content. Even if you turn to a designer, he will need to know how many different pages the site will contain, and what you want each of them to do. A good rule of thumb is to not have anything more than is absolutely necessary. This will save on loading time and keep potential buyers and fans from having to spend a ton of time trying to navigate your site to find what they are looking for. As always, keep things as easy and straightforward for people as possible, since the average persons attention span is very limited.

Along these same lines, you will definitely want to avoid various annoying features such as a video introduction or music that plays in the background while people are browsing the site. Avoid anything that scrolls or flashes. These things were cool back in 1995, but not so much now. If you find a web designer that recommends any of these things, I would strongly suggest looking elsewhere. Their main concern should be to make sure the site is functional in all popular web browsers to include tablets and mobile phones. They should be able to advise you on design, but ultimately the content choices will be up to you.

What kind of pages should you have?

Any band website should include these basic pages:

Home Page: This is where visitors will land when they type your site's address into their browser. It should contain links to all of your other pages, and be reasonably nice to look at. Be careful to not include things that take a whole lot of time to load, since people can get impatient and decide not to bother with waiting. Having a picture of the band and an indication of what you are all about on this page is probably a good idea.

About Page: This page tells the reader who you are and what you do. You can include who is in the band, who your influences are, where you have played etc. Keep it as short and to the point as possible.

Media Page: This page should have some videos or sound clips embedded in it. Obviously, videos would be most desirable. Choose some of your best material and you will be all set.

Download Page: If you have music available for sale (iTunes, Amazon etc.), you should probably have a separate page linking to the download sites. Include as many sites as possible, since not everybody uses iTunes.

Shop Page: This is where you can put your online store to sell various merchandise you may have such as T-Shirts, hats, CD's etc. If you don't have anything to sell right now but it's something you want to look in to, check out CafePress. You can use their site to design a wide variety of different items that will be printed on demand when people order them. This way you don't have to keep any up front stock, and you can still make a decent profit when people order the items you designed.

Contact Page: This is the most important part of your website. You might want to have your web designer include a form here so that people can insert their information easily and just press send. Another option is to have only a link that when clicked, will bring up a default e-mail box for the person to write their message in. Whatever you do, don't just list an e-mail address and expect a person to copy and paste it. Make it easy.

You may also want to consider adding a phone number to your contact page if at all possible. There are various sites on the Internet where you can buy an inexpensive toll free number, and these always look very professional. Not too many people in today's world will want to pick up the phone and call you in lieu of sending an e-mail, but it's always best to give them the option.

These are of course just the bare basics that you will want to use when getting a website started. If you want to get a little fancier, you can add a section just for band member bios, a download page where people can get wallpaper or print out flyers to help you advertise, or a page where fans can post their own photos that they took of your band at a performance. Just remember not to get too crazy and clutter everything up. In the case of a website, less is usually more.

Other Social Media

If you haven't done so already, you will definitely want to get your band a Facebook and Twitter account. Depending on what direction you want to go and how much you want to get involved with your fans, you may also want to start an Instagram account as well, which will give you another place to post photos. Your web designer will be able to integrate these accounts into your website for you so that they will be visible to your visitors as soon as they land on the page. In any case, you will want to make sure to provide links to these accounts somewhere on your website where people can easily find them.

Part V. - Hitting The Road

On the road..where the night is black
On the road..where you don't look back
There's a white light in the distance, where it's goin'
nobody knows
If it's anywhere you'll find it...on the road.

Lee Roy Parnell, 1993

The Approach

At this point, you have your online presence all ready to go, and have also printed up some advertising materials. Maybe you decided to go the commando route and just burn your demo to a blank CD and stick it in an envelope. Either way, you are going to actually have to go out and try to get people to hire you with whatever you have. Depending on the venues you want to play, you will have to figure out whom to talk to. As we mentioned earlier, bars are pretty easy. All you have to do is go in during the afternoon and find the owner. You could also choose to call the venue and ask who is in change of booking the bands and what the best way to contact them is. Most places will probably be pretty used to getting these calls, so they will immediately know who to send you to.

When you finally find the right person, you will just have to rely on confidence in your product and some general social skills. If you have followed this guide, you should have a product that you are pretty proud of and know that you are ready to go. Shake hands, explain to the owner that you are interested in playing at their club and hand them your CD. This is pretty much all there is to it. You will be surprised at the amount of times the guy will just say OK and ask if you can play next Friday night. Trust me, it happens.

One word of advice would be to try and find out a little bit about the bar or club you are trying to play at. It doesn't make any sense to try and sell your Latin Dance band to a place that has a Toby Keith tribute band on the marquee for Friday night. I have been in the situation once or twice where the person booking the bands didn't pay any attention to the type of music we played. That night wasn't very fun.

Negotiations Etc.

Once the buyer decides to give your band a chance, he will probably come right out and explain to you how the pay works. If he doesn't, now is the time to ask. There are a few different pay structures clubs might use, so we are going to try to cover them all here to give you an idea of how they work. Also, remember that there is always a chance that a buyer might want to bring you in on a trial basis for the first show and see how you do. You might end up doing that first show for a reduced rate, but you will be getting your foot in the door. When you are just starting out, it's important to play as many shows as possible. With this being said, you should also NEVER allow yourself to be taken advantage of. Sometimes you do have to walk away from a bad deal.

One way you might get paid is by **playing for the door**. Basically, you and the club owner decide on a cover charge, and every person who walks through the door pays that amount. In other words, the amount of money you make is completely dependent upon how many people you bring in. For a band that's just starting out, this is probably the least desirable way to get paid since no one knows you yet, but you will probably have to accept it at least once in a while. This is one of the reasons it's so important to develop a good following early on. Advertise on social media, tell everyone you know and do whatever it takes to get people in the door.

If your band is playing for the door, be sure to discuss who the doorman will be with the club owner. Sometimes the club will provide one, but many times this will be your responsibility. Be ready for that, and find someone you can trust. You will most likely have to pay somebody to sit there and collect the money as it comes in, but it's better to have someone you know if at all possible. Having a random person collecting opens you up to someone stealing your money or letting people in for free. Obviously, you would do well to avoid these situations.

Another approach the club may take is just to pay you a **set amount**. This is pretty straightforward. You will agree on an amount before hand, and meet with the bartender or owner afterwards to collect the money. This can be a good scenario because you will know for sure what everyone will be going home with. At the same time, this can get frustrating if you draw a huge crowd and the club makes a killing that night. If the deal was for a set amount, you are pretty much out of luck.

A third option might be some kind of split that the owner is willing to do, or a combination of the above approaches. One of my favourites is agreeing on a set amount, say 300 dollars, and then the band gets the entire price of the door. This can work out to be quite a nice paycheck if you can a decent amount of people to the show. If you can get 100 people in at a 5 dollar cover, you will easily pull in 800.00 for a 4-hour show. This is great money for a band that's just starting out, and your fee can go up from there as you become more established. I've played shows where the base fee was 500 dollars or more, and what we collected from the door was just icing on the cake.

Comps

Occasionally, a club owner will explain that in addition to the money they are paying you, the band will be able to eat and drink for free. This is often used as an excuse to pay a smaller amount for the flat fee that we have been discussing. While this is all well and good, you have to remember to use caution and good judgment if you decide to drink alcohol while you are playing. Remember that you are being paid for what you are doing, and drinking on the job in any capacity is probably a bad idea. Whether it's offered up for free or not, always remain professional and exercise some self-control.

Along the same lines, make sure to avoid the dreaded Blues Brothers scenario at all costs. If you aren't familiar with the movie, this is basically what happens: The band comes in to play a show, and they end up drinking the whole time. At the end of the night when they go to collect their money, they are informed that their pay is 200 dollars, but they drank 300 dollars worth of beer. The lesson here is to always be aware of the drink policy, or you could find yourself actually OWING money at the end of the night.

Situations to Avoid

As you begin your adventure into playing live music, you will be faced with certain situations that you would do well to avoid. These are just a few of them that I have run into, but you are bound to find more along the way. In general, you want to question any gig that involves you playing for no money, and never under any circumstances pay money to play!

Playing at the occasional charity event or doing a free show for friends or family is one thing, but you should be very wary any time someone else asks you to play for free. Often times, bar or club owners might try to talk you into this because you are the new act in town, and they want to see how well you do. Do this at your discretion for possibly your first show ever, but there is really no need to do this after you have yourself established. If someone doesn't want to pay you anything for your time, there are plenty of other places you can go that will be willing to.

Even worse than free shows are the ones that people try and make YOU pay to be involved in. Believe it or not, this really happens. Most of the time, a hall or venue owner will charge a certain amount of money per band, and put them all on the same bill for the same day. As you might imagine, the bands that are willing to do this are all pretty terrible. This is definitely a major step down from playing for free, and should be avoided at all costs. If you are bad enough that you think people should be paid to hear you play, you need more practice. Head back to the basement and don't come out until your services are worth something.

You will also want to be careful before signing any type of contract with a venue. Paying a band to come in and play is almost always a cash transaction and no contract should be required to do this. My advice would be to avoid anybody that tries to get you to sign one. If you still feel like this is definitely a place that you have to play, you will want to get a lawyer to look over the contract before you sign it, just to make sure everything is legit. Even though Danny the keyboard player took a law class at community college and says everything is cool, remember that his opinion doesn't take the place of real legal advice.

Lastly, you will want to avoid booking shows with people you haven't seen or spoken to in person unless they have an established reputation. It's *probably* fine to set something up at Bob's Country Bunker if you have found them on the Internet and it's obvious this is a real place. It's probably *not* fine to set up a show with Damba Kibibi who calls you out of the blue to play at an old firehouse in Muncie, Indiana. Especially if you're based in Florida and he needs to borrow 500.00 to rent chairs.

Case In Point: Monaca Money

Around 2003, I was playing with a three-piece country outfit based out of northern West Virginia. We started out playing at a small bar in a Holiday Inn, but as the years went by, the operation got bigger and we began to command larger stages as well as larger paychecks. We played everything from bowling alleys to festivals and everything in between. In this band, the guitar player was our "leader" and therefore also acted as manager. He made a few good moves during those years, but some of them were pretty bad. This was one of those.

The guitar player booked us for an out of town show in Monaca Pennsylvania to play for a large crowd in a large hall. The promoter he booked the gig through was also promising a lot of money, so this guy went out and hired an additional musician (a steel guitar player) to give us an extra edge that evening. After all, we could afford it with the additional money we would be making.

Since we were traveling out of town to a place we hadn't been before, we showed up a few hours early to start setting up. The hall was indeed fairly large, and the seating was enough to hold a ton of people, just as the promoter had said. Things started to get a little weird though, when at about an hour until show time, there were only two people sitting in the audience. Three of us were very concerned, but the guitar player was certain people would show up soon.

Time kept on ticking by, and the rest of us began to ask questions. Where was the audience? Where was the promoter? As our pseudo manager, we had left this guy in charge of walking in, making the proper contacts and giving us the go ahead before we got the ball rolling on setting up for the show. He walked in and talked to someone, but apparently it was the wrong person. As we would later find out, the guitar player and the promoter had never met in person before, and made the deal for us to play the show online. Things did not look good.

By now, the rest of us decided to approach the people who were currently running the establishment. They explained that as we came in the front door, the guy who was promoting the show (who it turns out didn't work for the establishment) ran out the back door. He was kind enough to leave us something for our time though. As a matter of fact, there were four bags...one for each person in the band. By this time, it wasn't very surprising to find that we had been paid in CIRCUS TICKETS.

Needless to say, the three of us were very upset, and the guitar player was just confused. He made several attempts to get a hold of the promoter by phone during the most awkward and angry breakdown session I have ever been a part of. Surprisingly, the guy actually picked up at one point, and promised he would pay us in full. All the guitar player had to do was meet him the next day in a casino parking lot. Seriously. He said he would be the one "in the glasses" and would have the money "in a paper bag". The steel player asked our guitar player if the promoter indicated that there would be code words involved or if the money would be thrown from a moving vehicle. He didn't get the joke, no one ever heard from the promoter again, the steel player never played with us again, and we lost out on potential earnings that day from a real, paying show.

The lesson here is that you always need to be aware of whom you are dealing with, where you will be playing, and who will be paying you. This is a crazy, cash business full of liars, cheaters and scam artists. My best guess is that this promoter neglected to actually promote anything, and it didn't take him too long to figure out that nobody was going to magically show up to fill the seats. Even though this incident was no fun to be involved with, at least we didn't lose any money. This is yet another reason why you never pay anyone money for your band to play anywhere.

A Few Words on Advertising

With the show booked, you are going to want to make sure that there are as many people in the seats as possible, even if you aren't playing for the price of the door. Having a large amount of people come out not only makes you look better to the owner and makes it more likely that you will be rebooked, but it's also a lot more fun playing to a room full of people rather than empty seats. We have discussed a few ways of getting more people to come out, but there are some additional things you can do as well.

Besides your family and friends, the people you can rely on most are the ones who normally come to that bar or club anyway. The week before the show, the management is likely to put your band name up on the sign, but it would help to take this a step further. You should take the time to make up a flyer using Photoshop, Word, or some other computer program. Include an interesting photo of your band if you can, and include all the information about the show including the date, time, venue etc. Don't forget to include addresses to your website and social media either.

A flyer I made for the same 90's band in the other examples

You can always go around sticking these up on telephone poles, but this probably won't do much good. A better way to approach it would be to print off a stack of them and head out to the venue you will be playing. Ask the bartender if they would mind putting one on all the tables and a couple on the bar the week leading up to the show. If they look busy or untrustworthy, offer to do it yourself. Since they will want as much business as possible, they will most likely be happy to help. In all the years I have been doing shows, no one has ever had any objections to doing this.

Aside from just posting something on your own Facebook page or band page, you can also create an event on Facebook and actually invite people. Make it an open group so anyone can RSPV. Post links to this page on your other social media sites and do whatever you can think of to get people to commit. Once one person says they are going, other people are going to see it and check it out. Before you know it, you can have a snowball effect that results in people you don't even know saying they will show up.

Day of the Show

So now the show is booked and it's come to the day of the gig. Before you even leave the house, there are some matters you probably want to consider. Since you will be in front of a lot of people and representing yourself and the band as a whole on stage, you will want to take some time to choose what you are going to wear. No matter what style of music you are doing, you will want to dress the part, since that's probably what your audience will be wearing as well. If you play in a country band, buy a nice hat and a pair of boots. Jimmy Buffett tribute band? Try a Hawaiian shirt. You can see where I'm going with this. Before you leave the house, make sure to print up enough set lists for everybody and toss them in your bag.

You might also want to think about the fact that before the show even begins, you will likely be hauling a ton of equipment off a truck. If you have some really nice clothes that you want to wear for your performance, you probably don't want to get them torn and covered in sweat before you even start playing. For that reason, I advise you to carry your performance clothes separately, and wear something older and more comfortable to unload and set up in. Get changed back stage or in the bathroom prior to the doors opening for general admission.

Since it does take a while to set everything up, you will want to allow yourself plenty of time to get to the venue, get everything unloaded and hook it all up. Factor in some time for a sound check, last minute instrument adjustments and potential problems, and you are looking at getting to the gig at least two hours in advance. As you become more experienced, this amount of time may not be necessary, but I would advise playing it safe in the beginning.

As soon as you arrive to the venue, you should introduce yourself to whoever is working and let them know you are with the band that will be playing that evening. If you need anything unlocked to bring your gear in or if there is a special entrance you need to know about, they should tell you about it at this point. With your introductions out of the way, start bringing stuff inside.

Once everything is unloaded, in position and set up, you will want to begin a preliminary sound check. Hook up a CD or MP3 player and turn it on as you get your basic levels and make sure all the speakers are working. Having some music playing will also help decrease any stress that you might be experiencing, as well as providing some entertainment to the folks who are at the bar early in the evening.

Once all the speakers are working, it's time to move into the sound check. Have everybody plug in and start getting some levels. Make sure to have someone walk to all different parts of the room to hear how it sounds. Everything should sound good from all different areas in the audience. Keep readjusting the levels until you are happy with the way everything sounds. At this point, tune everything up, make it look nice, and get ready for the show. Keep the music on the stereo playing all the way up until you take the stage.

Part VI. - Showtime

Where's the feeling gone?

Will I remember this song?

The show must go on...

Pink Floyd - 1983

The First Set

You're here. This is what you have worked for over probably the last few months, and it's about to pay off. If you're feeling a little bit nervous, take some ease in knowing that you have done the groundwork, practiced hard, and earned the right to be here. You may feel a little bit uneasy for the first few songs, but it will wear off after that. Try not to worry too much about people judging you. You probably sound better than you think you do, and most people don't know enough to tell the difference anyway.

The most important thing to concentrate on at this point is trying not to move too fast. The adrenaline is bound to kick in, and you will want to speed everything up. Try and fight that. Think about everything you're doing, and don't be afraid to talk to the crowd and engage them. At the same time, do not let them dictate your show. It's definitely a bad idea to hand out copies of your set lists or place them out on tables. People will start yelling songs at you, and you will be forced to either ignore them or become a glorified jukebox. You have your set lists made up, so stick with them.

Whoever the front man is should definitely be talking to the audience between songs. Saying things like "we're glad to be here!" and "remember to tip your bartenders" is always a good way to get comfortable doing this. If all else fails, you can rely on the old one-liners like "don't drink and drive because you might spill your drink, and that's alcohol abuse." Just kidding. Don't do that unless you are seriously strapped for something to say.

If you find yourselves running too fast, stick in some songs from the last set. If you are forced to play something over later, it's ok. We are talking about several hours between the first and last sets, so you will probably have an almost entirely new audience with people coming and going all night. Even if people have been hanging around, they will probably be too drunk to remember that this is the second time they have heard "Run Through the Jungle". People will likely be asking you to replay songs at this point anyway, so don't worry too much about it.

When you go to take your breaks, remember that you always want to have some type of music playing. Most of the time, the band will have an MP3 or CD player plugged into the board and play music from that. Obviously, the selections should be songs from the same genre you are playing but not anything that you will be playing that evening. In some bars, the management will turn the jukebox up during breaks. If you are unsure, ask the bartender before you go on for the evening.

Before going on a break, be sure to let the audience know what's going on, and that it will only be a short time before you will be back. Breaks should generally be about 15 minutes, so a simple "we'll be back in 15 minutes" will be just fine. This should probably go without saying, but do keep a close eye on the time. You don't want to keep the audience or the management waiting too long for you to get back on stage. When you're ready, fade out the music and get back to it.

Breaks will also provide you with an opportunity to replace strings, re-tune guitars and fix other problems. You should NEVER have to stop a performance for stuff like this. It's a good idea to make sure guitar and bass players know how to play with a broken string, and that the drummer has plenty of extra sticks within his reach. I've thrown more sticks accidentally than just about anybody, so I know what I'm talking about here. Having a second guitar ready to go is also a great idea, and is absolutely essential for any player who isn't 100% comfortable with the idea of playing an entire set with a broken string. If push comes to shove, you can always take an early break, but this should be a last resort. I've actually finished playing a song while the entire house drum set collapsed in on itself, so there is no excuse.

You should also be taking some time during breaks to talk to the audience. There are probably going to be several people at the show who want to request a song, compliment your playing or maybe even ask to book you for a private show. Try not to be all weird and standoffish, since after all, these people did pay to come here and see you play. If things get too weird (and they sometimes will, trust me), take some solace in the fact that you can play the "oh look at the time, gotta get back on stage now" card anytime you want.

Breaks should also be the only time you are ever getting drinks from the bar, unless of course you have someone bringing them to you. Some establishments will provide you with free drinks or some sort of tokens that you can redeem for them. As previously mentioned, make sure you consume these with moderation and common sense. If you can't drink too much or you are a raging alcoholic, you're going to need to stick with water or soda. It's best for everyone involved.

Case In Point: F@%# the Police

Sometime around 2009, I was playing with a alternative rock group. The band was still in its infancy, and we landed a show at a local club. I had played there several times before, but it had been a few years. We all felt pretty well prepared for the evening, but as soon as we started unloading the gear, things took a turn for the weird.

It wasn't long before we were approached by some guy who was obviously strung out on a few different kinds of drugs. We were still a few hours away from the show starting, so that meant that this guy started his evenings quite early. Like 4 o'clock early. He introduced himself as a "sound man" and claimed to be friends with the owner (which everyone does). We'll call him "Jake the Snake".

Jake the Snake then proceeded to rattle off a laundry list of unimpressive local bands that he had supposedly run the soundboard for, and presented us with a ton of terrible business cards. Despite the fact that several members of the band had played at the club before, he thought it would be nice to give us a few "pointers" on how things "usually run around here." Instead of offering advice on the acoustics or recommending a nice 24-hour diner, he told us that it was "fine to do coke in the bathroom" but to make sure that we "smoked our crack in the car." Needless to say, we were pretty appalled, and the guitar player let him know it by asking something like "who do you think we are?" That part was pretty funny.

Before Jake stumbled away, he did offer one sage piece of advice. He explained that since the bar was close to a residential neighborhood, that occasionally there were complaints about the noise level. As such, the police were regularly in and out of the place, and had become friendly with the staff. Besides making sure to take their drugs in the appropriate places, all Jake asked was that the band didn't start any trouble with the police and turned the volume down a bit if they were ever asked to do so. Who could argue with that?

Day turned to night, and lots of people came out to see the show. Everything had gone pretty well for the first set. We had avoided all major disasters and the sound quality was fairly decent. Three of the four of us, however, would notice things start to take a turn throughout the second set. The singer (who wasn't that great to begin with and had trouble memorizing lyrics...he did buy the PA system though) was starting to slur his words and totally forget how to play his rhythm guitar parts.

Perplexed, we walked to the bar and someone ordered a drink.

When whomever it was attempted to pay, the bartender looked confused and explained, "that's what the tokens are for." Naturally, we asked, "what tokens? We didn't get any tokens, did we?" I'm sure you can probably see where the story is going from here. Apparently, the singer had somehow intercepted a large amount of these things, which were intended to be distributed between FOUR adult men for drinks over a four-hour period. We had just reached the halfway point in the show, and the singer had managed to consume an amount of alcohol that would have landed Ozzy in the emergency room. For the first two hours, this guy had his girlfriend going back and forth between the bar and the stage, running booze like Chalky from Boardwalk Empire.

Obviously, things just got worse from there, and the singer absolutely lost his mind. About midway through the third set, we shut his amp off on him, and he was too drunk for the rest of the show to notice. Additionally, Jake the Snake had given us three rules, and this guy broke at least two of them (probably all three, really). The police did come in that night and asked us to turn the volume down. Instead of complying, this guy ran to the PA system and turned everything up louder.

Then, in a stunning move even for this guy, he decided to change up some song lyrics. He had forgotten the real ones anyway, so I'm sure he didn't think it would matter very much. With at least one uniformed member of law enforcement present, he began to yell "F@%# the Police" and "F@%# the pigs". It was some of the most bizarre stuff I'd ever heard from a stage. We managed to cut that song short and get through the rest of the show with everybody else picking up the slack. When we got paid for the evening, the singer gave all of his money back to the bartender in exchange for what he called "road beers", and he took a homeless man back to his place for an "after party". I hope he had fun, because that was it for him. I walked off the stage that night and said "never again". I never did see him after that, but was inspired to include this story here after somebody told me that he was finally famous, and made my old hometown newspaper. It was, of course, in the police log after he was arrested.

The End of the Night

When it comes to ending the show, you should be aware of the time and when last call is going to take place. Most of the time, the house lights will come up, but don't take this for granted. Make sure you know what time you are supposed to stop playing. Thank everybody for coming out, and don't forget to plug your next show, your website etc. Put your instruments down and take time to talk to the remaining crowd and mingle for a few minutes before you start packing everything up. This will probably take a while until you establish some kind of a system. Take your time, and make sure to prevent damage to your gear by doing it right.

After all that's out of the way, it's time to start the re-loading process. As lots of guys already know, packing a truck or a van with a ton of different stuff is an art in and of itself, and takes precision placement. All that's left to do at this point is change back into your normal people clothes, find the person in charge and get paid. Congratulations. You have just completed your first paid performance!

Collecting Your Money

This brings us to the matter of collecting your paycheck at the end of the night. This should be a pretty straightforward process. Chances are, the actual owner of the establishment will be at home and long asleep by the time you finish packing up your gear. So, your main point of contact should be the bartender unless otherwise specified. Most of the time, they will approach you to bring you the money, but don't be shy about approaching them about it if you have to.

Obviously, you will want to count the cash and make sure everything is as it should be. If there are any disputes, such as the amount being less than you agreed upon, every effort should be made to resolve the issue right then. Since you don't have a contract with these people and we are talking a relatively small amount of money, this is your best chance to make things right. In all my years of playing, a discrepancy such as this has only happened once or twice. Most of the time, the establishment was willing to correct the error. In the event that they aren't, you have a few options.

If you have an established relationship with the club, you can always come back and talk to the owner in the morning. If not, you might insist that the person in charge call the owner immediately to clear up the situation. Since they probably don't want to do this, they will most likely pay you so that you can be on your way. This will probably result in a damaged reputation with the venue, but if they have a problem paying you the money you agreed upon, you don't really need to be playing there in the first place.

Another option would be to call the police. I have never had to do this myself, and I don't imagine things will ever come to this for you either. Most of the time, venues will want to make every effort possible to avoid having the police at their establishment. This might be just enough of a threat to make them pay you and let you go on your way. Obviously, don't call the police on yourself if you or your band mates are drunk, and only call if you are certain you actually have an argument.

Sometimes, you need to firmly insist (in the nicest way possible) that you be compensated for your efforts. Along these lines, you can always take some items from the establishment in a sort of "barter". If a club or bar has been unable to pay, I have always been willing to accept an even trade. This would be considered an extreme situation. Over the last few years that I was playing out heavily, I acquired drink-ware, glass bar mirrors, vinyl banners, tap handles, non-slip rugs and even road cones in lieu of full or partial payment. A friend of mine has received entire crates of whiskey and a pinball machine to settle up his paychecks. Don't let yourself be taken advantage of.

The manager of the bar will most likely end up paying you in 10's and 20's, and occasionally some 5's and 1's slip in there. Obviously, it's the bandleaders' job to pick up and disperse the cash amongst the band. As with anytime cash is being flaunted about, try to do this in a semi-private location. Probably not on the corner of The Boulevard and Convention Center Way at 3:30 AM. It's always faster and a bit more professional to pre-count the money for everyone if possible, especially with larger amounts. This avoids standing around in a circle like cartoon characters who have never seen money before, handing out one bill at a time in the "one for you, one for me" style. I guess it doesn't matter, but just a little tip that I thought I would pass along.

This should also go without saying, but when you get your money from the club owner, make sure to check that it's real, and that it's all there. You probably shouldn't insist on him standing there while you count in front of him (unless he's a proven thief or something), but always do a quick thumb through to avoid any problems. I have heard more than one story with a band being paid in a roll of cash that turned out to be a 20.00 bill wrapped around a wad of monopoly money. It happens. There are a lot of greasy, con-artist weirdos in this business. And I love them all.

Making Extra Money Through BOR Sales

I thought that some information on this particular topic might be of major interest to bands that want to make as much money as they can at each gig. This topic could probably cover a whole second book (who knows, maybe I'll write it someday), but I didn't want to hold any good ideas back here. So what are BOR sales? Simply put, these are items you sell in the "back of the room", hence the name. Merchandise can range from anything from T-Shirts and hats to CD's and digital download cards. The possibilities are endless. Once again, use your imagination here.

You might have used my previous suggestion about having a print on demand style Cafe Press store on your website. That's great, but the stuff you sell at shows should definitely be all together different. This is for a few reasons. First of all, Cafe Press and similar web sites are very convenient since you don't have to keep any stock of the actual items or come up with any money for upfront costs. If someone buys your item, you get a small but reasonable royalty for designing it, and the customer has become a walking billboard for you. It's a winning situation in that context, but it wouldn't be at all if you had to pay full retail price for this stuff to bring to your show and sell. Also, it's nice to have some things available at live shows that can't be purchased anywhere else, and maybe things that aren't easily made by an on demand printing company.

Your best solution in this case would be to shop around at a local or online quick run T-Shirt print shop and have some shirts printed in common sizes. T-Shirts are probably going to be your most commonly sold item, but it's also nice to have the one size fits all idea that you might get from hats or whatever. Keep in mind that you will have to carry all this stuff around, so you want to make sure you only have "the good stuff". Oh-so lightweight download cards are your friends here. You will also want to invest in a case of some kind to keep all this stuff in, that can also double as a sales point or counter top, and probably an iPhone or Droid app that allows you to accept credit cards as payment.

One last thing to keep in mind is that you will need someone to run these back of room sales. So, unless you have a bored wife or girlfriend who doesn't mind constantly sitting with this stuff, that's going to be money out of your pocket, just like with the doorman. Maybe you can even arrange for one person to do both if necessary and the venues layout allows for it. A second option would be to only sell merchandise during your 15-minute breaks, or just at the end of the show. This would be a last resort option, as we have already discussed in previous sections what you should be doing during that time.

Rebooking the Club

As long as everything has gone smoothly up to this point, there should be no reason to hesitate in asking for another booking or two. In most cases where the band is at least a moderate success and the owner or booking person is still around, you will be booked for one or two dates for the following weeks or months. Occasionally, you will have to stop by when right person is around or when the manager has his date book available. Don't forget to follow up on this stuff, as establishing good relationships with clubs that pay decent and that you like to play at is really the secret to being happy and successful in this business.

If the manager brought you in on some sort of trial basis (paying your band less than he pays the other acts since you were new), now is also the time to remedy that situation. Don't be afraid to bring this up. You have held up your end of the deal, brought in a decent crowd that didn't tear the place up, and acted professionally. A club owner can't really ask for more than that. At this point, there should be no reason for them to pay you any less than the average going rate for live acts in your area.

This would also be the best time to try and get some kind of testimonial from the manager, if you should choose to seek one. The show is currently fresh in their mind and everybody is standing right there, so strike while the iron is hot. A lot of established bands might not really need to get these, but they can be a major help in the beginning as something to list in promotional packs or on your website. If you are trying to book other area shows in similar establishments, it never hurts to have a positive review from the competition.

Some Final Thoughts

After reading through all of this information, you should now know exactly what it takes to go from starting a band all the way up to getting your first paying gig. If you do the things we covered, it's probably going to be pretty difficult to not be at least moderately successful. Your particular level of success will be directly correlated to the level of effort you put into all of this, and how much of your time and patience you are willing to dedicate. A successful musician or a band is not made over night. Even if you have a good idea of what you are doing going in, there will still be bumps in the road. Get through the early ones, and you'll find you have what it takes to make it as far as you want to go.

There are plenty of people in this world who will tell you that you can't make any money, let alone a living playing music. They might say that the odds of any kind of success are very small or that you should think "realistically". These things are often said by talentless and very boring people who are content to spend their lives in a cubicle or behind a counter somewhere making money for other people. Be thankful that you have the talent and drive to give this music thing a shot. As I mentioned in the beginning, since you are the kind of person who seeks out advice and resources, you are already miles ahead of a ton of other people who would like to be doing the same thing, but are scared or aren't willing to ask for help.

As with everything else in life, there are no magic bullets or guarantees of success. The closest thing that I can offer you, and maybe the most valuable thing written here in this book is this: *go out and do it*. This might sound deceptively simple, but it's absolutely true. The only thing standing between you and having your own band that's out and making money (or doing whatever else for that matter) is YOU. Make the commitment, take the first step, and don't look back.

Part VII. – Resources

Finding Members:

themusicianfinder.com - bandmix.com - bandfinder.com

Advertisement Printing:

gotprint.com - vistaprint.com

Blank Media:

newegg.com - amazon.com

Disc Printing:

discmakers.com - groovehouse.com

Website Design:

wordpress.com - wix.com - iwebtemplate.com

Recording Software:

audacity.sourceforge.net - acoustica.com - avid.com

Cover Song Licensing:

harryfox.com

Supplemental Books:

The Social Media Magician by Dan Sperry:

penguinmagic.com/p/S17227

Author's Material:

notafew.com - youtube.com/imageten –

allenabbottmagic.com

Download Industrial Refuse by Not A Few on iTunes or
Amazon today!

The author would like to thank the following:

Special thanks goes to my friend Jeramie Gorman with whom I have written many songs and shared in many adventures. I wouldn't have made it this far without you. To Josh "The Boy Wonder" Durst and Rob "The Greatess" Alatis who shared in more crazy nights and stories than most people could have hoped to be involved in over an entire lifetime of music. To Bill McKeen for being a great teacher, friend, and the best guitar player I have ever met. Many thanks also to Dan Sperry, Sergio Chaparro, Michael Doane... and of course, Dave. You gave me my start, and created a monster.

www.ingramcontent.com/pod-product-compliance
Lightning Source LLC
La Vergne TN
LVHW051239080426

835513LV00016B/1660